for Relevance

THE SCHOOLS

AND SOCIAL CHANGE

HOUGHTON MIFFLIN COMPANY · BOSTON

NEW YORK   ATLANTA   GENEVA, ILL.   DALLAS   PALO ALTO

TO

EARL S. JOHNSON

Colleague, scholar, great teacher, and friend

Education

CARLTON E. BECK

NORMAND R. BERNIER

JAMES B. MACDONALD

THOMAS W. WALTON
University of Wisconsin-Milwaukee

JACK C. WILLERS
Auburn University

Editor's Introduction

THE SOCIAL FOUNDATIONS of education grow increasingly important in the education of teachers for today's society. The areas of history of education, comparative education, philosophy of education, cultural anthropology, and educational sociology are always basic to educational thought. But in a time of international stress, of complicated racial relations and of urban dilemmas, and in an educational setting characterized by conflicting values and controversial curriculum decisions, the social foundations become crucial.

Each area of the social foundations has potentially a major contribution to make to the relevance of our educational enterprise. Yet the student's time is limited. So the potential contribution of these fields is increased by bringing to bear the knowledge of scholars of the several foundational fields within the confines of a single book. Both the undergraduate student who has not yet taught and the graduate student, who often has taught, should profit from a synthesis of ideas and insights derived from scholarship in the broad field of the social foundations.

To make such a contribution to the reader, *Education for Relevance* was prepared by a team of collaborating scholars in the social foundations. As members of the Department of Social and Philosophical Foundations at the University of Wisconsin at Milwaukee for a period of time, the authors became well acquainted with each other's specializations, concepts, and ways of working. Their competencies as a team embraced the broad area of social foundations. So they decided to combine their abilities specifically to produce this volume. Their book is not a compilation reprinted from other sources.

Sometimes the reader will be sharing historical insights, sometimes philosophical, sometimes sociological, sometimes comparative,

v

sometimes anthropological. Always he will be seeing the work of education as it looks to students of the social foundations. A unifying thread running throughout the book is the commitment of the authors to an education which is relevant to educators and their endeavors in a rapidly changing society. The end result should be more relevant contributions to students and their lives through the teaching of those who read and use this book.

WILLIAM VAN TIL

Preface

THE THESIS OF THIS BOOK is clearly that education, to be anything important, must touch the lives of men; hence the title,
Education for Relevance.

Every society attempts to perpetuate its values and action-commitments. As societies become more complex, a more formal attempt to do this is made. Thus the phenomenon called education
arises. But social conditions do not stand still; they are dynamic,
changing. Ways of educating that were successful in transmitting
cultural values and action-commitments in the past may lose their
effectiveness in a changing world. They may become anachro-
nistic; they may lose relevance in the lives of men.

There are many factors in modern societies, and especially in
America, that tend to increase the irrelevance of formal education.
It is our contention that to combat such irrelevance we must understand its origins. What we believe to be the chief factors that need
careful attention have been discussed in this book. We have attempted to bring to bear recent findings from the social sciences
without merely repeating or summarizing such findings. There
will be few footnotes, since the chapters are primarily essays representing what we consider *most relevant* to an understanding of
our society and its problems.

Verbalisms and pedantry are not education, nor is an ornate
building, nor a highly structured code of laws concerning how
children shall spend their time. Meaningful education must make
contact with cultural values, social functions, and individual lives.
To do less makes education irrelevant in a world that cannot afford
any more irrelevancies.

Past outlooks and procedures may offer some guidance, but no
tradition can be assumed to be correct and effective at all times for

all men. A tradition must be "present-tested." If it proves to be worth keeping, it is not because of its history, but because circumstances have not changed enough to render it irrelevant. This is not to say that it will always remain so, or even that this tradition is the *most* relevant or meaningful procedure today. We believe with Thomas Edison: "Once you solve a problem, begin right away to find a better way."

It is imperative that man ask the right questions, the pertinent ones. This seems the only real way to promote further significant thought and to stay abreast of the unique features of every era.

Education, then, is not a matter of past answers, impressive structures, or attractive materials. All of these may or may not play a part in truly touching the lives of men. We believe that the leaven of the daily bread of education is relevance. It is with this in mind that we have written our book.

Dr. Beck is the author of Chapters 1, 2, 3, and 10; Dr. Walton, of Chapter 4; Dr. Bernier, of Chapters 5 and 6; Dr. Willers, of Chapter 7; and Dr. Macdonald, of Chapters 8 and 9. Because of multiple authorship, there will be some significant and genuinely differing points of view, which are not only unavoidable but desirable. In the consideration of such complex problems, more than one conceptual scheme provides fruitful avenues to analysis and understanding. We view this as a strength, not a weakness.

We wish to extend our appreciation to our typists, Wilma Foreman, Carol Jacobson, Marcia Powers, Merrillan Meurer, and Lee Saltzman, whose help was invaluable in meeting deadlines, to Mrs. Rita Collins and Mrs. Shirley Kersey for invaluable aid in selecting art work, to our families, who always must lose some priority in any writing project, but most of all to our students who — above all else — have done the most to keep our own work relevant.

CARLTON E. BECK
NORMAND R. BERNIER
JAMES B. MACDONALD
THOMAS W. WALTON
JACK C. WILLERS

Contents

PART TWO · *Education in a Changing World*

PART ONE

Historical Perspectives

Preach, my dear Sir, a crusade against ignorance;
establish and improve the law for educating
the common people. Let our countrymen know
that the people alone can protect us . . . and
that the tax . . . is not more than the thousandth
part of what will be paid to kings, priests, and
nobles who will rise up among us if we leave
the people ignorant.

THOMAS JEFFERSON

"Every child must have the best education this nation can provide."

Lyndon B. Johnson

Chapter One

THE PURPOSES OF
AMERICAN EDUCATION

Every society in recorded history has sought to perpetuate itself and its values. Formal education is only one way of doing so. Although the major focus of this book is the school, we must define education much more broadly because many social groups compete, complement, and influence value formation in our society. Each group has its own ideals and attitudes, its own sets of desirable and undesirable behaviors. Education, then, is not merely the program of the schools but *any planned, orderly changes in behavior conceived by a social group and intended to perpetuate its values and action commitments.*

We recognize that there are many phenomena in life that affect one's outlook and behavior which are *not* orderly and are *not* planned by social groups (e.g., earthquakes, droughts, accidents). Though it could be argued that these unplanned happenings also represent a form of "education," they are of only tangential concern here. The *intentional, purposeful* workings of groups in the shaping of others is our focus. As societies grow larger and more complex, inter-group conflicts become a significant force in every man's life. A society can ignore the nature of such value differences only at its peril.

3

A Brief Overview of American
Educational History

America's unique position in the contemporary world has been made possible largely through the educational progress of many dedicated men and women whose ideas represented departures from the goals, concepts, and methods of their time. Our concern in this chapter is with (1) the goals, concepts, and methods of various periods of our educational history, (2) the turning points which challenged older ways of thinking, (3) the reasons for such challenges, (4) the direction taken as a result of each "new" way of thinking about education and society, (5) the consequent gains and/or problems to our society and to individuals and groups at each turning point, and (6) the succeeding stages of educational development in the United States to which these gains and problems led.

Perhaps some brief statements of educational purpose from men who represent the various periods of our educational development will set the stage for our examination of American educational history. They are taken, respectively, from the Puritans (specifically from the wording of the "Old Deluder Satan Act"), from Benjamin Franklin, from Thomas Jefferson, from Ralph Waldo Emerson, from Theodore Roosevelt and from Boyd Bode. Although many other quotations might well have been chosen, the following will serve to represent the temper of the times and the changing commitments of schools in our society.

The "Old Deluder Satan Law," enacted by the Massachusetts Bay Colony in 1647, required each town to make basic educational facilities available to its children:

> . . . It being one chief project of the old deluder, Satan, to keep men from knowledge of the scriptures . . . so that the true sense and meaning might be clouded . . . , that learning may not be buried in the grave of our fathers, it is therefore ordered that every township . . . shall then forthwith appoint one within their town to teach all children . . . to write and read . . .[1]

---

[1] Quoted in E. P. Cubberley, *Readings in Public Education in the United States* (Boston: Houghton Mifflin Company, 1934), p. 15.

It was the duty of the parents and of the community, then, to
see that each child was able to read his Bible so that his life
would reflect the values and action commitments of his religion.
Obedience to God, hard work, and frugality were among the virtues sought.

In an address delivered before an abolitionist society in Pennsylvania in 1789, Benjamin Franklin stated his educational aims
or purposes as follows:

> . . . To instruct, to advise, to qualify . . . for the exercise
> and enjoyment of civil liberty, to promote in them the habits of
> industry, to furnish them with employments suited to their age,
> sex, talents, and other circumstances, and to procure their chil-
> dren an education calculated for their future situation in life;
> these are the great outlines of the plan which we have adopted
> and which we conceive will essentially promote the public good
> and the happiness of . . . our hitherto too much neglected
> fellow-creatures.[2]

Although these remarks were intended as a statement of Franklin's goals for the education of Negroes, they typify his educational
outlook for the common man in America during his day. Indeed,
it was the founding of Franklin's academy in Philadelphia in
1751 that provided the first real challenge to the religion-and-
classics oriented Latin schools of colonial America. His conception of education for livelihood and a satisfying life will be discussed later in this chapter as one of the true turning points in
our educational history and one which made good sense to the
average citizen. To the common man before this time, education
was formal in a literal sense; it was education *only* in *forms* —
forms of verbs, forms of nouns, forms of classical style — none of
these even remotely resembling the only "form" which made contact with him, the form of life he was likely to lead. Though
the so-called "Academy Movement" of the late eighteenth and
early nineteenth centuries departed in many ways from Franklin's
original, practical intent, the breakthrough charted the course for
a more life-oriented education.

Jefferson, too, recommended the extension of education to all

---

[2] Benjamin Franklin, in *The Works of Benjamin Franklin*, ed. Jared
Sparks (Boston: Whitmore, Niles, and Hall, 1856), pp. 515–516.

people but stressed the differences of men far more than did Franklin. To Jefferson, to speak of educational opportunity made far more sense than to speak of "equal education for all." He believed in offering education in the liberal arts to any child who proved himself capable of learning and dealing with the high level abstractions involved in such an education, regardless of whether or not the child was able to afford it. He felt, too, that those students who were not academically talented must be educated for useful pursuits so that the nation might benefit from their labors and so that they might also become participating citizens in our form of government. These views are well expressed in the following excerpts from a bill Jefferson introduced into the Virginia legislature in 1779:

> . . . whom nature hath endowed with genius and virtue, should be rendered by liberal education worthy to receive, and able to guard the sacred deposit of the rights and liberties of their fellow citizens, and they should be called to that charge without regard to wealth, birth, or other accidental condition or circumstance; . . . children whom nature hath fitly formed and disposed to become *useful instruments* [italics ours] for the public, it is better that such should be sought for and educated at the common expense of all, than that the happiness of all should be confided to the weak or wicked. . . .[3]

On another occasion he spelled out clearly the goals for which he deemed such education pertinent: "The general objects of this law are to provide an education adapted to the years, to the capacity, and the condition of every one, and directed to their *freedom and happiness.*" [Italics ours][4]

Jefferson envisioned at least literacy training for all citizens so that all could, to some degree, handle their own business affairs and partake of citizenship in an informed way. Beyond this, however, he advocated an "aristocracy of talent and intellect," with the stated understanding that those who showed early potential for

[3] Thomas Jefferson, quoted in Gordon C. Lee, *Crusade Against Ignorance* (New York: Bureau of Publications, Teachers College, Columbia University, 1961), p. 84.

[4] Thomas Jefferson, quoted in Robert Ulich, *History of Educational Thought* (New York: American Book Company, 1950), p. 248.

leadership should have an education which would prepare them for their responsibilities, viz., liberal education.

In the decades immediately following the death of Jefferson in 1826, Ralph Waldo Emerson and other Transcendentalists considered seriously the problem of what sort of education would best befit their image of the truly educated man. In 1863, Emerson said:

> . . . A treatise on education, a convention . . . a lecture, a system, affects us with slight paralysis and a certain yawning of the jaws. Education should be as broad as man. . . .
> . . . We teach boys to be men such as we are. We do not teach them to aspire to be all they can. We do not give them a training as if we believed in their noble nature . . . facts . . . skills . . . words . . . we aim to make accountants, attorneys, engineers, but not to make able, earnest, great-hearted men. The great object of education should be commensurate with the object of life. It should be a moral one; to teach self-trust; to inspire the youthful man with an interest in himself . . . to acquaint him with the resources of his own mind . . . to inflame him with a piety towards the Grand Mind in which he lives. . . . A man is a little thing whilst he works by and for himself, but when he gives voice to . . . love and justice, is godlike . . .
> . . . We learn nothing rightly until we learn the symbolical character of life.[5]

This strong statement was the true beginning of the transcendental-idealistic strain in education in America. The Transcendentalists stressed man's proper relationship to a Divine Power but pointed out that man must examine himself, to try to see the Divine working in and through himself. The emphasis on love and justice for all men melded with Lincoln's freeing of the slaves and the larger movement of political and social progressivism which manifested itself in many social justice measures and "improvement" movements. Once again, the answer to implementing equality of opportunity and acceptance of men previously considered social inferiors was to be "education." Following the great

[5] Ralph Waldo Emerson, "Education," in *Emerson,* ed. Mark Van Doren (New York: Viking Press, 1946), pp. 254–255.

influx of immigrants in the decades just preceding and following
the turn of the century, a first-order-of-business status was given
to "Americanizing" immigrants, freed Negroes, and others through
the public schools.

With the outbreak of World War I soon after the turn of the
century, the attempt to create a set of "American values" for all
citizens moved abruptly into an enthusiastic nationalism. Several
events in our history and in our educational history, especially,
indicated that patriotism was to become the cornerstone of education for the first four decades of the twentieth century. This spirit
is typified by Theodore Roosevelt's statement that

> It is an evil thing for any man of education to forget that educa-
> tion should intensify patriotism, and that patriotism must not
> only be shown by striving to do good to the country from within,
> but by readiness to uphold its interests and honor, at any cost,
> when menaced from without."[6]

In an article published in 1908, he added that there must be a
partnership between the Department of Agriculture and other
branches of the federal government with the schools to assure that
our equality of educational opportunity and our national strength
and readiness would become a reality: ". . . our system of public
education must be broadened . . . instruction relative to the
farm, the trades and the home . . . [the school system] should
be aimed primarily to fit the [majority of students] for actual life
rather than for a university."[7]

This spirit of "America first" was heightened during World
War II but after the War was met with opposition from intellectuals and statesmen who voiced the fears and hopes of millions in
a world which had begun to realize the possibility of total anni-
hilation by atomic and hydrogen bombs unless people of all races
and nationalities learned to live together peacefully. And once
again it was to the schools that our statesmen turned to implement
their ideas. Instead of following the thinking of Roosevelt (and,

[6] Theodore Roosevelt, quoted in *Readings in American Education,* ed.
William Lucio (Chicago: Scott, Foresman & Company, 1963), p. 30.

[7] Theodore Roosevelt, "The Emancipation of Education," *Good House-
keeping,* 47 (November 12, 1908), p. 626, as reported in *Readings in
American Education, ibid.,* p. 24.

incidentally, that of the early founders of the guidance and counseling movement) of finding man's place in his society and suiting
him for it through education or training, we chose another course
of action. One could find many quotations from twentieth century writers to express it. If we take into account the fact that
"Progressive" educators viewed "society" as much larger than "nation," the words of Boyd Bode, a leading Progressive educator,
provide the theme of the sixth period of development: "We do
not educate an individual for *a* place in society, but to enable
him to find his own place."

If one couples this statement with John Dewey's clear call for
a new orientation in education, one can see clearly that education
is to be (1) for all men, (2) transcendent of national boundaries,
(3) a vital force in bringing order to the ever-shrinking globe,
and (4) man's only hope in the face of ever-increasing rivalries
based on selfish, narrow goals. In his famous *Democracy and
Education,* Dewey says,

> One of the fundamental problems of education . . . is set
> by the conflict of a nationalistic and a wider social aim. In Eu-
> rope . . . the new idea of the importance of education for hu-
> man welfare and progress was captured by national interests
> and harnessed to do a work whose social aim was definitely nar-
> row and exclusive. The social aim of education and its national
> aim were identified, and the result was a marked obscuring of
> the meaning of a social aim.
>
> . . . Science, commerce, and art transcend national boun-
> daries. They are largely international in quality and method.
> They involve interdependencies and cooperation among the peo-
> ples inhabiting different countries.[8]

The two quotations above point out the vital concerns of this
book. Education must not constrict; it must liberate. It cannot be
narrow; it must be "social" in the sense of developing sincere sensitivity for the plight of all men everywhere. It must be aimed at
expanding man's proprium to include broad experiences, unfa-
miliar ideas, and diverse cultural patterns. Whatever else it does,
it must do these things, or become irrelevant to life in the modern
world.

[8] John Dewey, *Democracy and Education* (New York: The Macmillan
Co., 1916), p. 97.

Six Periods of Educational Development

From the foregoing overview of our educational history, it may be seen that the purposes of American education may be divided into six major periods: (1) Education for Salvation, (2) Education for Livelihood, (3) Education for Productive Citizenship, (4) Education for Moral Inspiration, (5) Education for Patriotism, and (6) Education for World Society. Although these subdivisions are of necessity arbitrary and overlapping, as are any such subdivisions of history, they may prove helpful in understanding our educational development.

The overarching aim in all these periods has been "equality of educational opportunity so that ————— ," and the educational philosophers of each age have filled in the blank. The degree to which *complete* equality of educational opportunity — as we understand that phrase today — was advocated depended upon certain important social conditions which statesmen and educators evaluated. Education in seventeenth century Puritan New England was indeed Education for Salvation, and that alone; it was not necessary to extend educational opportunity to all citizens beyond the reading and writing stage ("religious literacy"); only those young men who showed great promise of being able to become ministers had need for learning beyond this simple level. And this is true of each succeeding stage we shall consider — that is, what was deemed desirable by the society was destined to be the aim of education. There has always been a lag or discrepancy between the ideal and the reality in any human endeavor, especially in education. But it seems fair to say that education mirrors the needs of society as seen by educational and political leaders. In other words, given a certain goal, that which moves us toward that goal has been considered good. This approach to living or to education has not gone unchallenged, however, for it bypasses any judgment of the appropriateness or morality of the chosen goal; it simply expresses the attitudes of those in position to make changes in education. This thesis will come to the fore again and again in the chapters which follow.

We shall turn now to some of the specific events which have had great influence on our educational system throughout our brief but eventful history as a nation. Again, we must return to our initial paragraphs. The following discussion of the six periods of American educational development is a history of planned, orderly changes conceived by social groups to perpetuate their values and action commitments. It is to these intentional, purposeful attempts at shaping education, and through it society itself, that we must give our closest attention if we are to understand education in American society.

1. EDUCATION FOR SALVATION

Since the dawning of civilization men have sought answers to their questions concerning their origin and their relationship to the supernatural. Men have always deemed it necessary to instruct the young in the beliefs and approved actions of the group into which they were born and lived. The primitive rites of tribes, especially at puberty, are only one example of the serious attempt of elders to perpetuate the values of the society through the instruction of the young.

Another example of this value perpetuation took the form of early Christian catechizing of prospective and novice members of the faith. To some degree this approach through formal teaching, whether done by clergy, laity, or self-instruction from books has typified all religious faiths. Every religion has its approved and disapproved behaviors and beliefs, its holy sources, and its commitments regarding man's relationship to his fellow men and to the deity. With this in mind, let us consider the Puritan settlements of seventeenth century New England, the true beginning of our nation and of our educational history.

The Puritan Mind. Those who settled in the northeastern section of what is now the United States were chiefly dissenters from the Church of England, those who had sought to "purify" it of what they considered serious errors and practices. Finding only persecution and little success for their efforts, these "Puritans" sailed to the New World in search of religious freedom and opportunity. Every American schoolboy has been exposed to the stories of the hardships encountered by the Puritans in their struggle to build a new life for themselves in the "New England." Our chief concern here is the type of education deemed proper in such a milieu and the way it came about.

The Puritan virtues of hard work, love of God, pious behavior, and devotion to the commands of the Scriptures were vital to our early New England settlers. Many of the leaders who arrived there in the early and mid-seventeenth century were well educated. These men, chiefly ministers, saw a need for developing two types of citizens: those who would provide leadership in this church-centered territory and those who would follow by carrying out God's commandments and attending to the daily labors of the communities. Indeed, it was the age-old problem of theocracies: what education befits the church and civic leaders? What education is proper for the laity? The answer chosen was the age-old answer; leaders should be educated in the Word of God and in the justification of the faith through the study of classics, ancient literature, philosophy, and the writings of earlier churchmen; for the common man, education was necessary only to the point of making him aware of the basic elements of his faith, so that he might live out his life in pious service to God and man.

The early Christians had accomplished this type of education by holding separate schools for the laity and the clergy. One example was the Benedictine concept of schools for the *externi* and the *interni,* the former being those who would "go out" (of the monastic schools where they learned the catechism and prayed) to resume life in the secular world, but as Christian believers, and the latter, those who were entering the religious life as monks, priests, nuns, or other clerical figures. The education of these persons was more extensive and dealt with the justification of the faith and its history. Early Christians reasoned that this was necessary, since someone had to explain to those of other faiths or of no faith just why Christians believed as they did. There was neither time nor facility to make of all Christians apologists for the faith, and therefore the two-function educational aims described here were followed. The common people were told that if questions arose which their catechetical knowledge could not answer, they should refer them to the clergy.

The Puritan faith arose at a time when trade, exploration, and manufacturing were on the rise, and when not only religion but the economy cried out for the literacy of all people, at least to some rudimentary but functional level. Following Martin Luther's teaching that even "If there be no Heaven and no Hell, each man must be able to read the Word of God," the Puritans set as their goal for the common man the ability to read one's Bible and/or prayer books and an understanding of the Puritan outlook on life and death. Literacy would serve a double purpose as time passed and as towns and cities arose in New England, but the original intent was the religious and moral training of believers who would carry on the faith. Obedience and submission to the will of God was the hallmark of the good Puritan layman.

The First Schools. For the clergy, the same idea which pervaded early Christianity was followed in New England. As early as 1635 a Latin grammar school was built in Boston, and only a year later Harvard College was established for the training of Puritan ministers. The prerequisite for entry into Harvard was an understanding of Latin and Greek, the languages of "the minister and the scholar."

The legal history of early New England Schools set important precedents for all of American education. As one reads of these developments, keeping in mind the context in which they arose, one sees a devout group of believers trying to transcend the many vexing and desperate problems surrounding them and to assure the continuance of their faith to posterity.

The first schools were patterned after England's method of voluntary schools. The townspeople would simply meet and decide to establish a school and to pay a schoolmaster. Laws in the late 1630's attempted to make the maintenance of a school compulsory for all towns of a given size, usually fifty families, but such laws either failed, were unpopular, or resulted in many arguments among the independent Puritans. Many of them remembered only too well the English Poor Laws of 1601 which established "education" by fiat for children from "bad homes," and they wanted no part of a trend toward government dictation in the area of education. The Poor Laws made possible the removal of a child from his home if, in the judgment of the court, the home was "bad" for children. Alcoholism, narcotic addiction, idleness, and many other conditions were given for such removals, but, whatever the reason given, the Laws were most unpopular among the common men. The child so adjudicated was apprenticed to a tradesman who was to teach him to read and write and to perform a useful trade. In return for these benefits, plus food, shelter, and clothing, the child was bound by legal contract to the master until a specified age under strict provisions governing his behavior. But many tradesmen proved unable or unwilling to be teachers of literacy skills, and children often were cruelly treated. Many child suicides, murders, and runaways were recorded, but the courts continued to enforce the laws because they viewed such "education" as the best available remedy for the current social ills. The feeling was that if a child were given a useful trade by which he could make his living, and literacy enough to understand the teachings of religion, he would be far more likely not to repeat the mistakes of his unfit parents. These ends are still popular ones today among those planning special educational programs for delinquent, underprivileged, or alienated youth, although debate rages concerning the means of attaining literacy, job skills, and moral behavior.

The American pride and belief in local control of education may be traced to the rejection by the Puritans of any "larger" government specifying the type of education their children should receive. Parental responsibility was an important theological as well as social commitment of the Puritans. Still, something had to be done to insure a steady flow of able students into the ministry, to provide for orphaned children, and to be sure that some minimal standards were met for all Puritan children. The first truly effective step in this direction was the famous "Old Deluder Satan Act" of 1647, referred to earlier in this chapter.

Administration of the Early Schools. "The Old Deluder Act" provided that the administration of the schools resulting from the law was to be under the jurisdiction of the local community. It ordered that communities of fifty families must establish a reading and writing school and that communities of one hundred families must establish a Latin school for the preparation of bright young scholars for college.

The law was not universally accepted, even though succeeding versions of it stiffened the fines for non-compliance, but gradually more and more towns set up schools, all under local control. Financing was typically done by tuition charges, public assessment, lottery, or other combinations of means. This law, often

A New England dame school, 1713

called the basis of compulsory education in America, was not, strictly speaking, just that. It was compulsory that schools be set up, but the enforcement of attendance was a local matter. It was not until the 1850's that education was made compulsory for all children through state legislation.

To the Puritans, "education for salvation" was the most important function a school could serve. Teachers were expected to instruct in religion as well as in literacy skills. Methods were basically catechetical and recitation-oriented. Discipline was harsh for malingerers. Indeed, there was much public credence in the phrase "beating hell out of children." A reluctant scholar often felt the rod, the only "sure" way of ridding him of that old deluder Satan.

Stemming from the same belief that salvation was important and that parents were to be held accountable for the religious instruction of their children, the Selectmen's Act of 1654 required that parental representatives chosen by ballot be responsible for overseeing the schools. These citizens were to be devout men who would not only hire teachers and make sure that good learning took place in a religious atmosphere, but also would control the expenditure of funds. This is usually viewed as the origin of our local boards of education. Again, the basic assumption was clear: the local people knew best what sort of education their children should have and how much they could afford to spend on it. The current debates, usually in a "civil rights" setting, about state and national "control" of education usually bring out references to the "intents of our founding fathers" concerning local control. It is true that this intent was there, but the context then was far different from what it is now. The religious homogeneity of the early New England villages and towns, as well as the racial homogeneity (not 100 per cent, however), left little need for debate on what "ought" to be taught, by whom, and to whom.

A Massachusetts Law of 1693 gave the Selectmen the right to place on the ballot their recommendations for school expenditures. If a majority voted in favor of a proposed budget, it became law. This systematizing of the finances of education removed much of the uncertainty and diverse means of support connected with earlier New England education.

By these laws and beliefs, then, New Englanders gradually established schools which were to set precedents for many decades to come. Education was to be publicly financed, locally controlled, and available to all. The curriculum and content were to be in the "common branches of learning" and in religion — the Puritan religion — which was deemed of utmost importance in all parts of the colonies. In communities where homogeneity of religious belief was the rule, few problems arose, but in areas where "islands" of different religious groups lived in proximity to others, the trend was toward separate private schools conducted by the various churches, sometimes with and sometimes without the use of public money. The so-called Middle Colonies between New England and the South were the best example of this. To have "religion" taught in school implied that it must be someone's particular brand of religion, and this would not be acceptable to all faiths. Objective teaching about religion or historical accounts of religion also would not be acceptable, since it was *not knowledge about* religion that parents sought but *religious commitment* and *specific credal instruction*. Recognizing this, Jefferson announced the doctrine of a "wall of separation between church and state" which meant essentially that no man should be taxed to support a religion not his own, and that education and other church activities must be supported by private, not public, funds. Jefferson wanted no control of religion by government, as had often happened in other lands when the "holders of the public purse" began to dictate limitations on religious matters, nor did he wish to have churches dictating public policy through education. He therefore proposed a system of public schools apart from and not dealing with religion. Religion was to him a matter for individual conscience; religious instruction, he declared, must come only from parents or churches, not from the secular public schools.

This "wall of separation" has been breached many times, and today is in what its proponents call "severe danger of crumbling" by the expenditure of public (chiefly Federal) funds for various purposes. The "breaches" referred to are the provision of public money for bus transportation for parochial school children; "shared time" programs in which parochial school youngsters study the so-called "secular subjects" at a public school for part of the day, but study history, literature, religion, and other "commitment and sacred" subjects at their parochial schools; some "released time" programs for religious instruction; and the purchase of textbooks for parochial schools, among other public and semi-public programs.

Those who today believe firmly in "education for salvation" and wish to have the benefits of parochial schools have often approached the matter of public money for such schools under what is termed the "Child Benefit Theory," i.e., helping children as children, not helping churches. The arguments often are bitter and almost ludicrous on both sides, with one side maintaining that a child who is given a free bus ride or a hot lunch at reduced cost will rush out and spend the resultant savings on a rosary or other religious object, while the other maintains that because the parents of parochial school children pay state and federal taxes, the schools their children attend are entitled to aid in education. The history of the wall of separation and the breaches of it are interesting in themselves, but cannot be discussed further here. The suggested readings at the end of this chapter can provide more detailed coverage and can suggest further sources and ideas for discussion.

2. EDUCATION FOR LIVELIHOOD

As mentioned previously, education has most often been criticized by parents and students as being remote from the daily life they must face, a life in which men work for a living. Gerunds and participles, Bull Run, binomial equations, the capital of Colorado, and other staples of the educational diet have little or no connection with the world outside the classroom. If there is any single word which typifies and describes the intent of all the chapters of this volume, it is the word "relevance." Today both educators and students want a "reality contact" between what is done in school and what is faced in life.

Benjamin Franklin recognized this problem in the early eighteenth century. When he set up his academy in Philadelphia in 1751, he declared that education ideally should include "all that is ornamental and all that is useful." But, he reasoned, since schools have only a limited time in which to teach a child, it becomes the proper and serious business of the school to select what is most essential for the child to learn. It must examine life — especially the life the child is likely to lead — and to prepare him to take his place in it. Since, for most men, work is a necessity, practical subjects ought to be included in the curriculum. Thus surveying, navigation, bookkeeping, and other subjects which had a demonstrable usefulness in Franklin's Philadelphia

One of Ben Franklin's many inventions was this desk chair, the forerunner of tablet-armed chairs used in classrooms today.

found their way into his curriculum alongside the more time-honored ones. Franklin's stress was on usefulness, and this to him meant that he should emphasize English rather than classical languages, that he must teach science — which to him represented man's greatest hope for economic well-being —and that modern foreign languages must be given a real place in education. No longer could men look to the wisdom of the past for answers to present or future problems, and no single culture had all the answers.

This shift from classic-centered education to more "relevant" studies which began with Franklin's challenge to the Latin schools continued to be found in laws such as those establishing land-grant colleges and has since been a part of many state and federal programs. Some examples of note are the Morrill Act of 1862, which provided federal funds for the establishment of agricultural and mechanical colleges, and the Smith-Lever and Smith-Hughes Acts, which provided for the education of agricultural and vocational teachers and for agricultural extension services (1914 and 1917). Since that time many federal actions have been taken to aid the "economic man," not only as a student preparing for an occupation, but as a consumer as well. Various services have been enacted by law to aid in counseling, testing, placing, and rehabilitating workers, with the end in view being the reduction, if not elimination, of unemployment, misemployment, underemployment, and unsatisfying lives.

This period of educational development has never really ended, but has merged with other larger conceptions of what education must be and has become only one part of education. Jefferson and others, who saw the need for a larger concept, altered Franklin's intent, and the nation entered the period called here "education for productive citizenship."

3. EDUCATION FOR PRODUCTIVE CITIZENSHIP

After the American Revolution and the resulting independence from England, several factors led to a change in emphasis in the schools. The diversity of our growing population, the religious heterogeneity, the cultural differences, and the often grandiose expectations of immigrants could have had disastrous effects if our educational views had not been revised. Earning one's livelihood

was only one aspect of living. Learning to share in the responsibilities for civic affairs, to follow cooperative courses of action in running a business and in maintaining a new nation, to vote intelligently, and to share some portion of one's earnings for worthwhile public purposes were all quite as important.

No one, of course, wished to make the schools less "real" in preparing students for life's demands. The majority of them were still much too unrealistic, despite the admonitions of men like Franklin. What Jefferson and others were calling for was for what we may term "productive citizenship," i.e., a way of life which would produce socially concerned, literate, informed *citizens*, as well as either workers or scholars — the dichotomy which typified European thinking.

In order to realize this idea, Jefferson championed several educational reforms: (1) equality of educational opportunity (*not* identical education) for all men; (2) public support of bright but poor young scholars through whatever level of education they were capable of mastering; (3) local school districts which would assure the availability of education through the secondary level for those who were most able; (4) the creation of a public university where all common branches of higher learning could be studied without recourse to religious higher education (in keeping with his idea of separation of church and state); and (5) visiting teachers to mediate between parents and children when their educational aspirations differed, and to report to the parents the child's day-to-day progress as viewed by the teacher.

To Jefferson, such an educational picture would assure thinking individuals far better than would the "enforced morality" of church-sponsored education. Jefferson and others of his time placed hope in reason, in cooperation among literate men, and in dedication to the principles of freedom of inquiry, speech, and belief. This position created genuine antagonisms and hot debate between its proponents and certain religious leaders who held that the business of education was incomplete without the sanctions of religion and that the surest way to bring about the good life was to follow "God's Word." Rationalism was true to the temper of the times, but not universally accepted.

Perhaps because the majority of the people were not ready to

Thomas Jefferson contributed much to architecture as well as to education. His proudest work was his University of Virginia (Rotunda, 1872–1818, shown here), which exemplified both his concept of state-supported education and his love of Roman architecture.

place their faith in rationalism or secular citizenship — or perhaps because the schools were not able to make Jefferson's dreams a reality soon enough — another trend began developing in education. The spokesman for it was Emerson, although many men in public life, both in and out of education, championed the basis of the trend. It was what we might term here "education for moral inspiration." The mark of Puritanism's salvation seeking was involved in it, as was the concept of the value of satisfying work and a brand of self-reliance that was in tune with the frontier mentality, but it was also a search for something more than either of these concepts.

4. EDUCATION FOR MORAL INSPIRATION

This "something more" was wrapped up in the belief in what has come to be called the "American Dream." Scoffers are quick to point out that a dream is something unreal, something which vanishes when one opens his eyes, something that is only a pleasant game of wish-fulfillment, but not objectively true. Believers cite examples of men whose lives have been governed by the

21

CAUTION!!
COLORED PEOPLE
OF BOSTON, ONE & ALL,

You are hereby respectfully CAUTIONED and advised, to avoid conversing with the

Watchmen and Police Officers of Boston,

For since the recent ORDER OF THE MAYOR & ALDERMEN, they are empowered to act as

KIDNAPPERS
AND
Slave Catchers,

And they have already been actually employed in KIDNAPPING, CATCHING, AND KEEPING SLAVES. Therefore, if you value your LIBERTY, and the *Welfare of the Fugitives* among you, Shun them in every possible manner, as so many *HOUNDS* on the track of the most unfortunate of your race.

Keep a Sharp Look Out for KIDNAPPERS, and have TOP EYE open.

APRIL 24, 1851.

This poster was written by abolitionist Theodore Parker, a member of Emerson's circle, to warn Negroes of opportunists who received fees under the Fugitive Slave Act for returning runaway slaves.

underlying principles of the American Dream and see a greater America emerging as more and more men accept as their own life-style the brand of living it advocates. What constituted this dream?

Emerson and the other Transcendentalists spoke for many who denounced the tight rule of Puritanism, yet yearned for the virtues of hard work, for a proper relationship with God and with one's fellow men, and for the orderliness which obtains when men live "right." Coupled with this order seeking and relationship seeking was a belief that man has a purpose on this earth and that it can be realized and rewarded only if he simplifies his wants, lives closer to nature, and relies upon himself. Emerson did not seek God in creeds, but hearkened rather to an individual relationship with Him, to a respect for nature as His handiwork, and to aspiration as the keystone of man's existence. The aspiration of which he and others spoke (especially in such sayings as "Hitch your wagon to a star . . .") was not that of worldly gain and wealth, but a sort of striving which in itself had something holy in it and was a part of God's plan for man. Transcending the

ever-present world of things and events was not easy, and knowing what God wanted for each individual man was not just a
matter of following creeds, but both were part of man's highest
task as a creature of a Divine Power, a Grand Designer.

Emerson's ideas, as quoted on page 7, were in the spirit of
those who were seeking their fortunes or at least their daily bread
in the new land, yet they also satisfied the basic religiosity of these
people. Somehow the American dream, or what is often called
the Horatio Alger myth, became entwined with Emerson's views
on man and education. The humility of Emerson's deepest feelings was joined with the ambition, rightfully conceived and not
pejorative, of Alger. To many generations of Americans, this joining represented what education ought to reflect. Men were seeking guidelines for action in an increasingly complex world. As
Civil War, abolition, Reconstruction, women's rights, and, later,
world leadership and alliances, coupled with the slow vanishing
of the frontier, changed American society, the guidelines that had
once seemed so safe and secure became clouded and amorphous —
or worse, irrelevant to life as it was lived day by day. Only some
combination of Algerism and Emersonian thought seemed able to
help men stand bravely and erect in the face of these changes,
and the schools were once again called upon to enlarge their frame
of reference and to rebuild American ideals.

From the lead provided by Emerson and his contemporaries,
American education embarked upon a form of idealism which attempted to embody the best from each of the preceding stages and
to synthesize them into "education for moral inspiration," the goal
being a regeneration of man's faith in himself as a part of God's
Grand Design. Man was to seek his purpose not only as a worker,
or as a soul to be saved, or as a citizen of benevolence and sensitivity, but as more than any or all of these; he was to seek meaning, over-all comprehensive meaning, in his relationship to the
universe. For the schools, this meant assuming all the previous
roles, while somehow building in synthesis. But the task proved
too formidable for the often undertrained and usually underpaid
teachers, and education for moral inspiration often became plati-
tudes, preachments, or sterile examinations of the past. The great
gulf between what was considered education and what was considered training widened, and academicians began an either/or

dialogue which has continued in essentially the same fundamental form ever since. This was clearly not the intent of Emerson, but bookishness and isolation marked much of educational theory and practice well into the twentieth century. This remoteness from life was severely challenged by the advent of the First World War and by the efforts of the early progressive educators, school psychologists, and school guidance workers toward uniting science and education during the first three decades of the twentieth century.

5. EDUCATION FOR PATRIOTISM

World War I brought with it an extreme form of national pride, purpose, and patriotism. After the victory, America was reluctant to go back to the relatively isolated existence of pre-War days. The "American Way" of freedom of speech, thought, and economic enterprise became reified, and almost deified. The "moral inspiration" idea moved rather naturally and easily into a rather general feeling in the schools and in the nation as a whole that because of our moral fiber and hard work, America was destined to lead the way to a happier world, either by example — as isolationists would have it — or by involvement in world politics. Some spoke of the "manifest destiny" of the United States; somehow America was the embodiment of all the good things in life. It would be unfair to say there was *no* evidence pointing in this direction, but it would be equally unfair to say that we had all the answers and had no serious problems. Nonetheless, many local communities passed laws or otherwise made certain that no "foreign ideologies" were to be discussed or allowed to creep into the schools. The German language was outlawed in some states. Loyalty oaths in various forms were required of teachers in the years that followed. Then, when the Great Depression of the 1930's descended upon America, and when many people began asking what had gone wrong in this best of all possible worlds, there was the almost inevitable reaction in defense of our country, its heritage, and its destiny. Those who questioned its premises in any way were called anarchists, socialists, communists, or worse.

The coming of World War II only about two decades after the First World War solidified this reaction, and by the end of

Theodore Roosevelt's intense belief in patriotism was exhibited by activities such as his participation in a Girl Scout scrap metal drive after his offer to raise World War I troops was rejected by President Wilson.

it, this feeling and its antithesis among concerned individuals resulted in a sincere split on whether the United States should participate in the United Nations or refuse to join, as it had done when the question of support for the League of Nations came up after World War I. Nonetheless, America had become a world power and a beacon to many underprivileged people the world over, while to others it was the symbol of what was called "imperialism" in its worst form. The problems over what stance the schools should take on patriotism, UNESCO, and other related matters reached their pinnacle in the McCarthyism of the early 1950's.

6. Education for World Society

The Progressive Movement in education was part of, or at least parallel to, the broader movement of political progressivism on the national scene. As education became more pervasive and as opportunity to obtain it became a reality for most Americans in the 1920's and 1930's, it was apparent that the highly selective, book-oriented, verbal type of education would be increasingly less relevant to the thousands of young people now in school — that it would be impossible to ape the selective, "high standards" approach of European nations.

Under the leadership of men like John Dewey, educational philosophers began to examine the nature of the learner, taking their cues from infant psychology and related studies in the scientific analysis of human behavior. Forward-looking men before and after Dewey had recognized a fundamental fact: our schools could not offer education for the life one was told and expected to live, as in the "education for salvation" period; they could not separate man the breadwinner from man the whole organism as had been done in the "education for livelihood" period; they could not look upon man as merely a creature who must "fit in" as part of a mosaic called "education for productive citizenship"; they could not allow the luxury of the high-sounding but often irrelevant "moral inspiration"; and they could not assume the "patriotic" position that we were a nation apart from the troubles of others on our planet. In other words, Americans could no longer merely accept the "givens" of the past, the commands of authorities of the present, nor the heady but often inert exhortations concerning our "destined" future. We were faced with the realization that between life and death there was to be only the meaning we, ourselves, put into it; that we, like our country, must define ourselves by our actions. But this simply could not be done by following previous formulae. Thus the stage was set for the present period, which we shall call "education for world society."

The emphasis of "modern" or "progressive" education was on relativism, change, adaptation, flexibility, individual differences, scientific approaches, controversial issues, critical thinking, community action, involvement, social sensitivity, reconstruction. In practice, of course, and in the hands of shallow thinkers and teachers, these terms have become only slogans with no substantive meaning in education. But in the hands of several generations of teachers, they have helped to bring about the realization that mankind is not divided into immutable units called nations which somehow must always be suspicious of each other and must seek advantage at the expense of other nations. Today, despite international tensions and the ever-present threat of nuclear disaster,

John Dewey associated the goals of education with the necessary social conditions for human freedom.

we are coming to realize that there are worlds beyond national borders and that the united efforts, the supplementing strengths of all nations are needed to build a better world.

But this vision of a world society demands the total re-examination of the goals, concepts, curriculum, and priorities of the modern school, great though its success has been in the years since "education for salvation" was its main concern. The "new math," "new science," "new social studies," and all the rest are but reminders of this fact; it is as if the fabled "Saber-Tooth Curriculum" were again being flung in our faces — why, indeed, teach tiger clubbing when the tigers are extinct? Why follow tried and true methods, goals, and concepts when the whole context is changed? The security to be found by denying that anything is really different is simply whistling in the dark. Schools must change and are changing from cultural vacuums, from ivory towers peopled with Dick and Jane and other cardboard characters, from verbal learning, from the detached viewing of current events as if they happened on another planet.

The present generation of teachers, contrary to the shallow rantings of our loudest and least informed critics, is the most educated, most highly trained, and the most socially involved group

of teachers since the founding of our country. Our schools, long
the last outpost of sheltered thinking and irrelevance, have never
produced such high-quality students in such great numbers. Isolated instances to the contrary, our schools and universities are
producing the ingredients for the most exciting and potentially
effective generation ever. We need not fear the new challenges.

In the words of Seneca, written centuries ago, "God divided
man into men that they might help one another." To perfect this
help, to share with other people of all nations what we have, hope,
and are is the seeming destiny of mankind in general and of education in particular. The following chapters, which concentrate
on various aspects of this hope for relevance and mutuality among
men and among nations, are dedicated to the idea that understanding precedes effective long-term action. It is our hope that
they will provide a framework for understanding the subtle relationships of school and society and will help sustain the faith of
educators in the great significance of their work in the exciting
years which lie ahead.

SUGGESTIONS FOR FURTHER READING

Beck, Carlton E. *Philosophical Foundations of Guidance.* Englewood Cliffs, N.J.: Prentice-Hall, 1963.

Beck, Robert H. *A Social History of Education.* Englewood Cliffs,
N.J.: Prentice-Hall, 1965.

Butts, R. Freeman. *The American Tradition in Religion and
Education.* Boston: Beacon Press, 1950.

———, and Lawrence A. Cremin. *A History of Education in
American Culture.* New York: Henry Holt & Co., 1953.

Cremin, Lawrence A. *The Transformation of the School.* New
York: Alfred A. Knopf, 1961.

———. *The American Common School.* New York: Teachers
College, Columbia University, 1951.

Cubberley, Elwood P. *Readings in Public Education in the United
States.* Boston: Houghton Mifflin Company, 1934.

Curti, Merle. *The Social Ideas of American Educators.* New York: Charles Scribner's Sons, 1935.

Drake, William E. *The American School in Transition.* Englewood Cliffs, N.J.: Prentice-Hall, 1955.

Johnson, Clifton. *Old-time Schools and School-books.* New York: The Macmillan Co., 1904.

Knight, Edgar W. *A Documentary History of Education in the South before 1860.* Chapel Hill, N.C.: University of North Carolina Press, 1949.

————, and Clifton L. Hall. *Readings in American Educational History.* New York: Appleton-Century-Crofts, 1951.

Monroe, Paul. *Founding of the American Public School System.* New York: The Macmillan Co., 1930.

Potter, Robert E. *The Stream of American Education.* New York: American Book Company, 1967.

Reisner, Edward H. *The Evolution of the Common School.* New York: The Macmillan Co., 1930.

Rippa, S. A. *Education in a Free Society.* New York: David McKay Co., 1967.

Ryan, Patrick J. *Historical Foundations of Public Education in America.* Dubuque, Ia.: William C. Brown Company, 1965.

Thwing, Charles R. *A History of Higher Education in America.* New York: Appleton-Century-Crofts, 1906.

Woody, Thomas. *The History of the Education of Women in the United States.* New York: The Business Press, 1929.

Someday is today.

Chapter Two

EQUALITY OF EDUCATIONAL
OPPORTUNITY RE-EXAMINED

Much confusion in education has come about from a misunderstanding of the nature of the term "equality of educational opportunity." Perhaps the most effective way to reduce such confusion is first to examine what it is *not,* and then to attempt to define it.

The phrase as typically used is a slogan, a selling point for some particular idea or project. Though these slogans may have an appealing sound, many of the offerings represented by them do little more than promote *in*equality of educational opportunity by advancing the interests of special groups at the expense of others. It is, of course, necessary to "give" in some areas of education in order to allot more financial aid and effort to others. In their cumulative effect, all such measures *may* approach equality of educational opportunity, but any given project taken singly can only be regarded as a possible contributor. Equality of educational opportunity, then, is *not* the eventual or even the intended outcome of all programs waving its banner.

The most common misunderstandings of the phrase by the "man in the street" are that it means the same education for all children — i.e., "equal education" rather than "equality of educational opportunity" — and that it represents a birthright. A moment's reflection on the former interpretation by any thoughtful person, however, would turn up key arguments for the unsoundness and undesirability of this kind of program, and the birthright idea would then become meaningless. If the same education were given to all, it would necessarily be never-ending in a world which has so much knowledge, so many specialized fields, and such diverse needs. Or it would have to be at such a low level that anyone could grasp it, which would make it impossible to disseminate the vast knowledge mankind has gained throughout the ages. Human abilities, interests, and talents vary so widely that any attempt to implement the concept of equal education for all would be ludicrous if not tragic.

A Working Definition

Equality of educational opportunity, then, is not sameness. It is *not* based on the belief that all men are created equal. It is based on the belief that each man is created different, and that each of these differences must somehow be brought out for the good of society. Education is the vehicle upon which many thinkers from Plato to the present have depended for the process of sifting and sorting talent. Everyone recognizes that human talents are different, and that these talents are not readily ascertained by inspection. Equality of educational opportunity, then, serves the purpose of finding talent wherever it may be. It is, in its simplest terms, the decisions and actions necessary to provide access to learning for all, *but not without regard for certain qualities and conditions.*

This working definition seems serviceable and accurate, yet it is open to criticism, as are all definitions of emotionally charged concepts. The words in italics are the ones which will be of concern to critics, but if we were to accept the definition without this qualifying phrase, so much of society would have to be so radically changed that one would hardly recognize it. And although the first impression of some might be to welcome such a change, a closer examination of its meaning would lead them to reject it. For serious men during all periods of history, other social values have been far more highly treasured than equality of educational opportunity. For example, if we were to remove all obstacles to the success of this concept, what would happen to other cherished traditions such as the right of private ownership, the primacy of parental responsibility for the education of children, and the parent's freedom of choice of the type of education his children should receive? And what would happen to our current research programs that are valued by so many? The former would have great difficulty surviving, and the latter would certainly lose out in the competition for funds, for it would require almost our whole national budget for many generations to come to bring about this access to learning. And if we were to extend this idea to all men everywhere, the magnitude of expenditure would become astronomical, and other worthwhile social enterprises would have to be drastically curtailed.

Although it could be argued that equality of educational opportunity would improve our world to such an extent that it would be worth any cost, such thinking is visionary and does not square with the multiple demands of social living. We should therefore face this realization: In the world in which we live and move, the *goal* of equality of educational opportunity, and not its ultimate attainment, may be impetus enough to build a better world, if not a perfect one. The "conditions and qualities" referred to in the definition above might include such politics and programs as would allow us to move closer to our goal most quickly, and with as little damage to progress toward other socially desirable goals as is humanly possible.

Without further belaboring of this definition, then, let us conclude that the concept of equality of educational opportunity presupposes three component parts as a minimum. First, the *decision* must be made by the people, or by their governmental representatives, that such a goal is desirable. Second, *purposive action* must be begun to bring it about. Third, *social policies* must be instituted which will allow progress toward the goal to continue.

The Decision Stage

Decision itself presupposes prior need recognition, but this will not be discussed here, since the nature of such needs are so varied. Once the decision to pursue "equality of educational opportunity" has been made, it becomes apparent that it is to operate only within certain limits. That this is necessary derives from the nature of the group making the decision. For example, if a given nation decides to pursue this policy, its decision is not binding on other nations, and thus its scope is initially restricted. Many nations have made this decision, and not all made it for the same reasons. There were many national goals, and many definitions, overt or covert, regarding what constituted a man and therefore who should be educated. For example, in ancient Greece, slaves, who were not considered to be men, were automatically excluded from education, while in other nations non-citizens or non-property holders were excluded. Yet none of these nations saw any injustice in their exclusions; the reasons for the decision to pursue this commitment determined in great measure who were to be excluded.

THE ACTION STAGE

Regardless of the restricting conditions or exclusions, or how they may appear to others championing the same stated objective, certainly actions are necessary in order to translate the concept into behavioral patterns. There are no absolute rules governing actions which would be universally sanctioned or universally disapproved, since the decision-making group determines automatically not only which exclusions and conditions are "fair," but also the "best available means" to accomplish the goal in the shortest time possible or desirable. Naturally, these means vary and have varied greatly from nation to nation and from time to time.

A representative democracy of necessity moves slower and with more regard for the sentiments of the people than does a totalitarian government. Another factor in the disparity of time often found in these two forms of governmental control and action is the tendency of totalitarian governments to make a clear distinction between policy making and daily operation. If the daily operation is carried on by those who can give full time to it and who are not expected to think too critically or to evaluate and defend policy, then the policy makers, who need not spend time on routine problems, can make decisions and see that they are carried out expeditiously. Admittedly, in totalitarian systems there is a natural disregard for the very real problems of others, which may cause bottlenecks and morale problems, but on the whole, the totalitarian educational system grinds efficiently and inexorably toward its current goal, whatever that happens to be.

Democratic societies, on the other hand, tend to follow the philosophy that all those who carry out the decisions must have some hand in the making of them, either directly or by representation. Since direct involvement is increasingly difficult in our modern world, representation is almost totally the rule. To provide the checks and balances necessary to safeguard the interests of all groups and classes of people who are represented, however, the democratic society often slips into the morass called bureaucracy. Although the shortcomings of the bureaucracy are legion — to mention two of the best known, it is a cumbersome form of representation and it often becomes in reality the representation of special interest groups — it must not be dismissed too quickly as either inevitable or lacking in any redeeming qualities. It does have two positive aspects: it creates jobs, and it moves slowly enough that decisions that are unwise or too hastily arrived at often may be averted simply because of the number of people who must know the intent and scope of the action contemplated. Nevertheless it can be argued that there are better ways to create jobs, and that wise decisions, too, may be delayed and perhaps emasculated by the bureaucratic process.

The importance for education of the remarks immediately preceding is that our original idea of local control of education has already undergone great modifications. Any local community, state, or nation wishing to further equality of educational opportunity within its borders should be aware of its presuppositions in decision making, and must weigh also the relative worth of the alternatives open to it.

THE SOCIAL POLICY STAGE

After the decision is made and the courses of action are decided upon, there is yet another stage in the pursuit, if not the total realization, of the goal of equality of educational opportunity. This third stage is that at which a society makes clear through its laws and their enforcement the general acceptance of the goal by the populace. This cannot come about by edict but takes place gradually. The differential rate at which the goal is accepted is chiefly due to the degree of social stress present and the power of the decision makers to convince the masses that the goal is worth the adjustments necessary to achieve it.

Legal policy may reflect only the predilections of the party in power. But a party in power need not remain so, and in human history there is clear evidence of a basic principle of social change: *When a law is enacted which exceeds the limits of custom, social strife will result.* If the law exceeds the limits of custom too greatly, or if non-legal or extra-legal actions of the party in power do so, a revolution will ensue. If the tolerance limits of the society are in transition, however, there may be only brief periods of overt strife, or the antagonisms may take subtle or covert forms. The problem of the policy makers, or of the party in power, is specifically whether the end in view is worth the social strife caused by extending the law beyond the limits of custom. If, in the best judgment of the policy makers, the extension is justified, the action is taken, but with the realization that measures must also be taken to lessen the inevitable strife and social disorganization.

The most obvious recent example is, of course, the 1954 U.S. Supreme Court decision that segregated education must be eliminated because it is unconstitutional. That same body had affirmed the doctrine of "separate but equal" education in 1896. The justices knew that this reversal would cause serious social problems, but they ruled that the law must go beyond the limits of custom because the principle it represented was important enough to justify the risks. The decision, action, and social policy requisites described above have been determined. Neither "racial equality" nor equality of educational opportunity has yet become a reality, but the goal has been set in that direction.

These three components, then — decision, action, and continuing social policy — are the necessary conditions for any planned social change of direction, or extension of direction. Keeping the history and the current and possible future effects of the 1954 desegregation decision in mind, if we apply these three concepts to the goal of equality of educational opportunity, it becomes apparent that (1) the decision to pursue such a policy is made for various reasons; (2) the manner of implementing the policy runs the gamut of measures from simple edict and violent force to simple announcement of "popular" policy; (3) the exclusion of certain groups or individuals from the application of the policy rests on certain widely varying presuppositions;

(4) implementation may be a long-term proposition; (5) implementation and/or the methods used in implementation may result in the overthrow of the policy makers if enough people are strongly opposed to the policy; and (6) a new social structure, resulting from the extension of educational opportunity to certain individuals and groups may create social imbalances which will lead to changes in other aspects of living.

History of Equality of Opportunity in American Education

"Religious Literacy" in the Seventeenth Century

During the seventeenth century in both Puritan New England and in Virginia (the "Education for Salvation" period of Chapter One) the decision regarding equality of educational opportunity was clear: there must be schools available to all, but the parents were to decide whether a child would attain "religious literacy" there or at home. It was also clear that little real effort was to be given to the "equality" part of our phrase, since the procedures used were predicated on the belief that some children must soon drop out of school and others should continue to and past the Latin grammar school level. The curriculum was unyielding; if

A Colonial schoolroom. "The curriculum was unyielding; if a child showed little potential for learning . . . he was given no further schooling.

a child showed little potential for learning what was taught and in the way it was taught, he was given no further schooling.

This was the "action stage," or at least one of the decisive ones, in the early schools of America. The "social policy" was written into church belief and legal code (see Chapter One, pages 11–17) and approved, through fear if not through true consensus, by the majority of the people. This is not surprising, considering the severe penalties for any sort of dissent in Puritan settlements, and considering that this was a relatively simple and quite homogeneous society. Much of the homogeneity was derived from the common English background and heritage (see Chapter Three for the characteristics of the gemeinschaft type of society). The occasional dissenters who wandered in soon moved on, or conformed, or were persecuted.

THE ACADEMY MOVEMENT

Adhering to the six periods of educational development as set forth in Chapter One, the period following "Education for Salvation" was called "Education for Livelihood." As was mentioned in Chapter One, these periods did not pass out of existence; they arrived, were modified, expanded, or took other forms, and became parts of succeeding stages of educational development. "Education for Livelihood" has been one of the hardiest of all American educational aims; it has persisted just as has the need for livelihood itself. Throughout our history, presidents and educators have time and again reminded Americans that the ability to be self-supporting is worthy of a man's best efforts, and that to provide equality of opportunity for him to do so is a priority item.

The first steps in this direction were taken by the challenge to the classical, Latin-oriented grammar school by Benjamin Franklin's academy, which included practical subjects and skills such as bookkeeping, surveying, and navigation. Though the academy movement later moved away from Franklin's original objectives, it was still instrumental in making clear the fact that Americans were a restless, practical, production-oriented lot, and that education which did not appear to them to be relevant to their world was written off as unworthy of much genuine time and effort.

An apprentice learns skills in a blacksmith's shop, 1874. "Education for livelihood has been one of the hardiest of all American educational aims."

COOPERATION AND CITIZENSHIP

If the second period of educational development discussed above seems to lack social emphasis, it is because most Americans did not see themselves as a part of a larger community (a common phenomenon discussed at length in Chapter Five). Only primary groups such as family and church were considered important in a social sense until the chain of events leading up to the Declaration of Independence and the formation of the United States of America began to take shape.

The third period, "Education for Productive Citizenship," as typified in the writings of Thomas Jefferson and others, was almost inevitable. Though it was perhaps an extension of Franklin's ideas rather than a departure from them, the emphasis of the period was on founding and preserving a new nation, one in which equality of opportunity was to play a vital role not only in education, but in all forms of economic and social life.

It is significant that the drafters of the Constitution of the United States did not see fit to mention education at all, although they did allude to equality and equality of opportunity several times. Did they truly feel that education was a state and local matter, or did they somehow sense that any mention of federal involvement in education would so displease the representatives

of the states that they would refuse to ratify the Constitution?
At that time, there was no money or power to do anything about
education on a national scale, and the founding fathers may have
felt that any aid given to education by the federal government
would have to be justified as coming under the "general welfare"
clause of the document. The priority item during this period of
our national development was the creation of a stable economy
and a commitment to cooperation and citizenship.

The ideal of equality of opportunity and the concept of a "literate citizenry" runs through all of Jefferson's writings on education. As literacy and citizenship skills took on new and important
meanings at various times in American history, educators and
government officials introduced methods of upgrading them to
make them relevant to the times. Some misguided efforts resulted
in only a narrow nationalism that defeated some of the aims of
the Constitution, but the educational purpose of this period was
clear: the encouragement of productive citizenship.

Some actions taken to further this aim were the founding of
state universities, first in Georgia, North Carolina, and Virginia,
and later in other states; the setting aside of land for schools in
the Northwest Territory; and the granting of funds to the states
for educational purposes.

The Search for the "Grand Design"

The fourth period of educational development, "Education for
Moral Inspiration," was a natural response to the thinking of the
times, as typified by Emerson and other Transcendentalists and by
the pioneers moving westward with the frontier. It was a time
when the "Grand Design" of the universe was being sought once
more, but in the practical world rather than in formal, stiff-necked
lectures and sermons.

The abolition of slavery, education for women, concepts of
government, and the future of our nation were topics being discussed throughout the land. Many great questions, such as how
best to absorb the increasing waves of immigrants from other
countries and what kind of posture to present to other nations,
were no longer academic. The simple society was changing
rapidly into a phenomenon unique in the history of mankind, and
national leaders realized that if the nation was to follow faithfully

One of the first state universities founded was the University of Georgia. The campus scene shown is from the 1830 period.

At Mount Holyoke, one of the oldest women's colleges in the United States, women studied the sciences as well as the humanities. At right, students are at work in a zoology laboratory.

in the ways our founders had intended, its people must be literate, concerned, and socially aware. The times called for neither a restrictive, blind obedience to theology nor a production-and-individual orientation. The productive citizenship of Jefferson was thought to be too narrow and too worldly, although a careful reading of his writings belies this then-common interpretation.

Besides the ubiquitous Bible-reading and inspirational stories of the lives of great men, young people were taught to search for the true, the good, and the beautiful in their own lives. These values were also the basis for several educational actions which furthered equality of educational opportunity, and the partial basis for others.

Schools called "high schools" began competing with, and later superseding, the academies in the early 1820's. The first one, in Boston, was for boys only, but just five years later another high school was built in the same city for girls.

Through the efforts of forward-looking educational pioneers such as Mary Lyon, Henry Barnard, and Horace Mann, coeducation became a reality. The first coeducational college was Oberlin, in Ohio, founded in 1837. In the following year, a college for women, Mt. Holyoke, was established in Massachusetts; it became the first of a series of high quality women's colleges dedicated to the usual pursuits of knowledge but cognizant of the particular needs of women. It was not until 1856, however, when the first coeducational high school was established in Chicago that the old tradition of separate facilities for the schooling of boys and girls was challenged.

Equality of educational opportunity received another major boost with the offering of free elementary education in Pennsylvania in 1834 and the founding of the first publicly supported normal school for the training of teachers in Massachusetts in 1839. These normal schools aided in the improvement of the lower schools and advanced the interests of teachers. The idea of a profession of teaching in the United States was conceived much earlier than this period, but it was not until the 1850's that organizations began laying the groundwork for improving education through united efforts.

The Lyceum Movement and the Chautauqua circuit performances also received their impetus from the search for inspiration and truth. These movements were quite popular; large audiences frequently turned out to be addressed or entertained by some of the country's leading speakers and performers.

Laws making schooling compulsory on a part-time basis were passed in the 1850's, first in Massachusetts, and later in other states, and in 1890 the first full-time compulsory attendance law was passed in Connecticut. Among the inspirations for these laws were child health considerations and the desire of socially concerned people to get the children of idle and uncaring parents into the schools for longer periods and to keep them out of the labor market, at least for a while.

During and after the Civil War, several measures were taken to increase equality of educational opportunity for the American Negro, who was now free, but often free only to starve and to suffer. Among the federal institutions created to aid him were the Freedmen's Bureau, which helped former slaves to secure an

Governor LaFollette of Wisconsin lecturing to an audience at Chautauqua, where people came for summer recreation and discussions.

education, to learn their newly established rights, and to find jobs, and two colleges for Negroes, Howard University and Hampton Institute, founded at Washington, D.C., in 1867 and Hampton, Virginia, in 1868, respectively.

Another influence in the growth of equality of educational opportunity was the Morrill Act of 1862, which provided land to each state for the establishment of agricultural and technical colleges and universities.

The whole spirit of this period of our educational development was that every man has a place in the Divine scheme of things, and that it is the proper business of law, education, and individual and group efforts to encourage each person in the pursuit of his unique hopes and dreams. The political movement of Progressivism, with its emphasis on the relationship between the individual and the larger society furthered this aim. Progressive Education, which came into being at approximately this same time, represented a beginning in breaking down the formalism and detachment of schools and colleges.

The Resurgence of National Feeling

The fifth period, "Education for Patriotism," may be viewed by some as not truly a separate period at all, but rather the inevitable result of national pride in our quick ascendancy in the world of nations, and of efforts to meld sectional feelings into one national feeling. The Spanish-American War also did much to bring into focus a certain pride in achievement.

As the quotation from Theodore Roosevelt in Chapter One (page 8) indicates, there was a strong sentiment that individual rights could be safeguarded best through patriotism, and that the stimulation of a patriotic attitude was the proper business of our schools. Roosevelt's interest in furthering equality of educational opportunity was manifested in his recommendation that the curriculum of the schools be extended to include more subjects of use to non-college-bound students.

As was pointed out in Chapter One, the coming of the First World War increased the spirit of patriotism but also instilled suspicion of other peoples. Isolationism and "100 per cent Americanism" in the form of anti-minority-group actions contended with the Progressive spirit under the banner of patriotism.

This primer, used in the North during the Civil War, is an early ex-ample of the stimulation of patriotism by schools. Note that in his zeal the artist even included a Revolutionary War captain with a 34-star flag.

But it was our fate to experience the Great Depression and another global war, plus the Korean conflict and the Vietnam dilemma, all within five decades of the close of World War I. No longer could a narrow nationalism prevail. America was in-volved with all nations in one of two courses of action: either building or destroying the world.

SCIENTIFIC ADVANCES AND INTERNATIONAL TENSIONS

From the 1880's until the present time, American education has reflected both the advances of science and the tensions of in-ternational problems, but after World War I these developments took on new meaning, as did the concept of equality of educa-tional opportunity. Where equality of opportunity had once meant equality for Americans, with the rest of the world some-how standing off in the distance, now it meant that an inequality or injustice anywhere is a potential threat to all men, including Americans. In the present period, "Education for World Society," there is not only the recognition that there are other lands and other peoples but that there can be no true equality of educational opportunity until it includes all men.

The vocational education movement began in the 1880's in order to produce the workers and skilled technicians necessary for our modern society of specialization, mass production, and division of labor. To assist the development of scientific agriculture and mechanical arts, three important acts were passed by Congress between 1914 and 1933: the Smith-Hughes Act, the Smith-Lever Act, and the George-Deen Act. These acts greatly extended the funds for vocational education and enlarged the concept to include selling and service occupations as legitimate federal concerns.

Also during this period (the late nineteenth century to World War II), several important studies of the status of education in the United States were made that were influential in changing our educational thinking and policies. Among these — all of which are studies in themselves of the growth of educational opportunity and are worthy of further consideration by serious students — were the famous Committee of Ten and Committee of Fifteen Reports (1893 and 1895), the Eight-Year Study of the Progressive Education Association (1941), and studies leading to the "G.I. Bill of Rights" (1944).

The Fulbright scholarships and fellowships for international cultural and educational exchange, which were instituted in 1948, took us a step further toward "Education for World Society," as did the establishment of UNESCO, the organization set up by the UN to further world understanding and to encourage universal education. Subsequent legislation such as the National Defense Education Act of 1958 and more recent federal legislation has stepped up the expenditure of funds for education and has legally committed the United States to a policy of strengthening education and increasing access to it.

SUMMARY

The ideal of equality of educational opportunity is still being pursued vigorously, but with a long way to go. A selected chronology of events which have tended to increase or have been intended to increase equality of educational opportunity is presented in Table 1. Each event is a story in itself and warrants careful study.

This Indian girl from New Delhi is a graduate student at the Massachusetts Institute of Technology. She is one of many students benefiting today from educational opportunities offered in foreign countries.

The Future of Equality of Educational Opportunity

Let us reflect for just a moment on what types of people an educational system of true equality of opportunity would have to encompass: the gifted, the mentally retarded, the visually handicapped, the culturally different, the deaf and hard-of-hearing, the speech-handicapped, the children of migrant workers, home-bound students, the emotionally handicapped, and many others who depart from the norm to such a degree that the offerings of the ordinary school would be ineffective or less effective than they must be to insure true equality of educational opportunity.

Let us talk sense about this concept and make of it much more than the slogan it often is. First, let us understand it. Though equality of educational opportunity is at the heart of countless arguments about needs, goals, means, and expenditures, we shall never *attain* it because it is not a *point* but a *process;* it is a *journey,* not a *destination.* Just as one does not *attain* happiness, but instead finds moments of it and experiences pride, pleasure, and satisfaction in the pursuit of it, so it is with equality of educational opportunity. We must face the unalterable reality that equality of educational opportunity is a metaphysical rabbit. It eludes us regardless of the speed with which we move or even our choice of vehicles by which to pursue it. But we can come closer to it by taking certain actions and certain vehicles rather than others. We can keep the rabbit in sight, and, short of catching it, which we cannot do, the important factors are understanding in which direction it is going, knowing whether the gap is widening or closing, and making sure that the thing we are pursuing is truly the same rabbit and not a decoy.

If we might for a moment grant that the attainment of equality of educational opportunity is impossible, since it is a process and not a point, then let us examine how to keep our elusive "rabbit" in sight, and how, in using the "art of the possible," we might narrow the gap, even if we cannot close it entirely.

The three basic approaches to narrowing this gap have been and are *legal, educational,* and *financial,* with some overlap in the three. All of these approaches have produced positive contributions as well as some failures. Law, as we have stated at the beginning of this chapter, can either reflect custom or go beyond it. Education can be realistic or remain aloof and comfortable in an ivory tower. Financial aid can alleviate human needs and free our potentialities for important pursuits, or it can be wasted and thus preclude the use of those dollars for vital, relevant purposes. We must use all three of these approaches to their best advantage. We must not set goals which are unattainable and then pursue them as if they will be attained with the next grant, the next law, or the next additional course.

In short, there is no magic called "equality of educational opportunity" or any other sort of opportunity. Man defines himself by his actions, but educators and others can aid him in finding himself and in finding meaning in his world by setting the stage for the fulfillment of as many desirable goals as possible, with whatever is at their command at this finite point in history. Such has been the dedication of some men in all ages. May their number increase.

TABLE 1

A Chronological Listing of Selected Events That Have
Furthered Equality of Educational Opportunity
in the United States, 1600–1967

Date	Event	Intent or Effect
1642	First education law enacted in Massachusetts	Required schools in communities of fifty or more families
1647	"Old Deluder Satan Act" (Massachusetts)	Provided for Latin grammar schools in communities of one hundred or more families
1654	Selectmen's Act (Massachusetts)	Provided citizen control over schools; forerunner of the local board of education
1693	Massachusetts Bay Law	Placed tax for schools on ballot; eliminated haphazard financing
1751	Founding of Franklin's Academy in Philadelphia	First real challenge to classic-centered curriculum; emphasized practical orientation
1785	State universities chartered in Georgia and North Carolina	First state universities; cost to students was low
1787	Northwest Ordinance	Provided land for schools in the Northwest Territory
1819	Supreme Court's Dartmouth College Decision	Assured freedom of religious schools from public encroachment; encouraged many churches to open more small colleges
1821	First high school for boys founded in Boston	More realistic curriculum; low cost; not highly selective
1826	First high school for girls founded in Boston	Extended secondary education to girls
1831	Lyceum Movement begun	Created lecture-discussion groups for adults
1834	Free elementary education established in Pennsylvania	Extended elementary education Opened doors of higher education to many poor children

TABLE 1 (*Continued*)

Date	Event	Intent or Effect
1837	First coeducational college founded at Oberlin, Ohio	Opened doors of higher education to women on equal basis with men
1838	First quality college for women established (Mt. Holyoke in Massachusetts)	Offered the usual subjects but was also cognizant of women's unique interests and needs
1839	First publicly supported normal school founded at Lexington, Massachusetts	Began teacher preparation to improve instruction and build professionalism
1852	First public law requiring school attendance part-time (Massachusetts)	Brought to school children whose parents had neglected their education; a step toward the elimination of child labor abuses
1856	First coeducational high school founded in Chicago	Began a more realistic appraisal of education in American society
1862	Morrill Act	Provided land for agricultural and mechanical colleges in each state
1867	Creation of a federal Department of Education	Collected and disseminated information on the status of education
1872	Supreme Court's Kalamazoo Decision	Set precedent for use of tax funds for secondary education
1874	Chatauqua Institute begun	Provided adult education through lectures and other types of programs
1876	First graduate school established (Johns Hopkins in Maryland)	Gave more students a chance to do advanced study (John Dewey was an early graduate)
1883	Correspondence university founded at Ithaca, New York	Made higher education available to many who could not attend classes

TABLE 1 (*Continued*)

Date	Event	Intent or Effect
1884	Baltimore Manual Training High School established	First complete industrial training high school
1890	First full-time school attendance law (Connecticut)	Brought all children to school for a substantial portion of the day
1891	Founding of International Correspondence School at Scranton, Pennsylvania	Extended special courses and basic schooling to those unable to attend classes, chiefly adults
1893	Publication of the Report of the Committee of Ten	Recommended changes in college entrance requirements; foreign language credits dropped as prerequisite
1895	Publication of the Report of the Committee of Fifteen	Recommended improvements in teacher training
1902	First publicly supported junior college founded at Joliet, Illinois	Established abbreviated post-high school work; practical courses as well as academic ones were given
1906	Alfred Binet's I.Q. test published	First of many attempts at scientific testing to aid in teaching and counseling
1909	Publication of Frank Parsons' *Choosing a Vocation*	Beginning of the guidance movement; approach was to "match" men with job requirements
1910	First junior high schools established in Berkeley, California, and Columbus, Ohio	Attempt to apply child study to teaching at the preadolescent level
1917	Smith-Hughes Act	Provided funds for vocational education
1918	Education by now made compulsory in all states	Made possible concerted planning and greater influence of education

TABLE 1 (*Continued*)

Date	Event	Intent or Effect
1918	Publication of the Report of the Commission on the Reorganization of Secondary Education	Formulated goals of secondary education in the famous "Seven Cardinal Principles of Education"
1925	Scopes "Monkey" Trial, Tennessee	Tested academic freedom in teaching about evolution; resulted in the repeal of many anti-evolution laws
1925	Oregon Decision of the Supreme Court	Upheld right of parochial schools to exist; prohibited forcing public school education on all children
1933	George-Deen Act	Greatly increased the federal money available for vocational education and added selling and public service as legitimate areas for support of educational programs
1941	Publication of the "Eight Year Study" by the Progressive Education Association	Results of comparative study of traditional vs. progressive schools led to wider acceptance of progressive ideas in public school classrooms
1944	G.I. Bill of Rights legislation	Entitled thousands of young men to pursue subsidized education after World War II; greatly increased college and trade school enrollments
1946	United States Armed Forces Institute made permanent part of the military services	Encouraged and enabled armed forces personnel to take courses and correspondence work
1948	Fulbright Fellowship programs begun	Enabled students and professors of many nations to study abroad

TABLE 1 (*Continued*)

Date	Event	Intent or Effect
1954	Supreme Court's Nonsegregation Decision (Brown vs. Board of Education)	Segregation by race in public schools ruled unconstitutional
1958	National Defense Education Act	Provided federal funds in generous amounts for improving various aspects of education, especially mathematics and the sciences, as well as teacher education
1959	Publication of James Conant's *The American High School Today*	First in a series of Conant's important critiques of American education; awakened interest of educators and the general public in more effective schools
1960–1967	Increasing legislation by the federal and state governments to provide financial support to "culturally disadvantaged" youth, such as Project Headstart, Volunteers in Service to America, the Teacher Corps, the Job Corps, Project Upward Bound, and others. Great increases in scholarship aid, fellowships, and loan funds. Also the many benefits of the Elementary and Secondary Education Act, the Higher Education Act, and Civil Rights Act of the mid-1960's, and other legislation during this period have pointed up the gross inequalities in educational opportunity and aided efforts toward abolishing them.*	

---

* A more complete listing of recent legislation for federal aid to education, along with a penetrating analysis of its implications, can be found in Galen Saylor's "The Federal Colossus in Education — Threat or Promise?" reprinted in Harold Full's *Controversy in American Education* (New York: The Macmillan Co., 1967), pp. 282–290.

SUGGESTIONS FOR FURTHER READING

Cremin, Lawrence. *The Transformation of the School.* New York: Alfred A. Knopf, 1961.

Drake, William. *The American School in Transition.* Englewood Cliffs, N.J.: Prentice-Hall, 1955.

Krug, Edward. *Salient Dates in American Education.* New York: Harper & Row, 1966.

Rippa, S. A. *Education in a Free Society.* New York: David McKay Co., 1967.

Ryan, Patrick J. *Historical Foundations of Public Education in America.* Dubuque, Ia.: William C. Brown Company, 1965.

PART TWO

Education in a Changing World

What is our life but an endless flight of winged facts or events? In splendid variety these changes come, all putting questions to the human spirit. Those men who cannot answer by a superior wisdom these facts or questions of time, serve them.

RALPH WALDO EMERSON

In Ghana, a curbside letter writer types letters for his illiterate customers.

Chapter Three

EDUCATIONAL

AND SOCIAL CHANGE

Among the most frequent statements of social and political experts (and of some not so expert) are those relating to the fantastic rate of change today. The popular magazines and newspapers are full of articles describing the shrinking world of the super-jet aircraft, the catapulting of stone-age societies into the modern technological world, the revolt of the young in many societies against conformist adults, and on and on. Increasingly one feels somewhat like an inexperienced surfer who, finally getting himself in position on the board for his ride on the thundering wave onto the beach, suddenly realizes he is the victim of an unmanageable force that is hurtling him forward, and that there is little he can do but try to remain upright.

As a result of such feelings of helplessness, many people in America today take the attitude described in the recently popular song, "Que será, será, Whatever will be, will be" — we cannot know the future and could do little about it if we did know. Such a fatalistic approach to life by rational human beings is not quite enough, however. If the lessons of the past two hundred years hold any truth at all, we ought to be able, through the use of our intelligence, to understand the nature of the forces bringing about the changes in our world and if not modify them, at least learn to cope with them and even to use them to our advantage. Human behavior is not wholly the result of external determining forces. Rather, man is, to a large extent, a choosing animal who consciously builds institutions to meet his needs. An extension of this idea is that man is thus a considering animal, and that his choices are, or ought to be, the result of reasoned consideration rather than mere arbitrary selection.

If this discussion has any meaning for mankind in general, how much greater significance must it have for those involved in one of the most basic of human institutions, education. A major purpose of this chapter is to emphasize that education, both in its formal and informal aspects, is at the heart of cultural change. It is not only a basic factor contributing to that change but also an extremely sensitive barometer of change. Without engaging in the almost useless debate of which is the more important, intelligent educators must recognize that the school is both an agent of change and an agent of cultural preservation. The facts indicate that to discuss the school as a mirror of the culture as opposed to its being a determiner of change is to ignore a vast amount of historical evidence which tends to support the idea that the institution of education cannot exist in any society without the interaction about which we have been speaking. Educational change must reflect cultural change as well as to *assist in* that change. If an educational system does neither, the result will be serious inarticulation between various segments of the society and serious social problems will result.

A Definition of Education

TRANSMISSION AND TRANSMUTATION OF THE CULTURE

The above concept leads us to a definition of education, which, though by no means all-inclusive, is nevertheless functional. Education is, in part, the process by which the young of the society are inducted into the culture. That is, it is the means by which the society hopes to convince its offspring that they should want what the adult population thinks they should want. This may be seen by some as unfair, but it is a well known sociological fact, if not just plain common sense, that there is no continuity of culture unless the young come to value what rational adults value. All education is, then, to some extent indoctrinative. But it is also the process by which the adult assists in the development of the critical skills of the young in order to make possible desirable modifications of the culture.

In other words, the task of the educational system in any society, in any time or geographical circumstance, is to one degree or another as Earl Johnson says, both the *transmission* and *transmutation* of the culture. Johnson emphasizes the point in discussing the role of the teacher:

> The teacher . . . is called upon to play two roles: one as priest, the other as prophet. As priest, the task is to pass on the culture in order that it may be continued and preserved. As prophet, it is to interrupt its continuity. These roles are inherent and in the nature of things: the spirit of conservation and the spirit of change. Nothing can be real without both. Conservation without change cannot conserve; change only is passing from "nothing to nothing."[1]

As this quotation makes clear, regardless of the degree of emphasis on either cultural transmission or transmutation, all educational systems must perform both services. No society is static. All societies are in a relatively constant state of modification — some rapid and some slow, but all changing some beliefs, attitudes, and institutions during given periods.

FORMAL AND INFORMAL EDUCATION

Closely associated with the concept of transmission and transmutation is that of *formal* and *informal* education. These terms may have been used in a slightly different context in other writings, but in this book the term "informal education" indicates that type of learning which takes place as a result of interaction between the learner and his parents, the extended family, peer group, or community at large, and "formal education" indicates

[1] Earl S. Johnson, *Theory and Practice of the Social Studies* (New York: The Macmillan Co., 1956), p. 30.

In primitive societies education is largely transmitted informally. The child learns the skills needed for maintaining life in the ways of this father-son hunting team in Bechuanaland.

the teaching of selected parts of the culture to the young by persons specially designated by the society to undertake such teaching. A child is being educated informally when he is learning from his father how to square a board, set a trap, or how to chew skins to make them soft enough to use as clothing. Much of such learning is the result of direct observation and imitation. In most preindustrial societies the basic type of education is informal. Generally, there is a particular location in which formal education takes place. This special place is not always designated as a school, however; it may be a place of religious worship such as a church, mosque, synagogue, or even a cleared spot under a tree.

It is important to make two additional points in this connection before we move on. One is that in both formal and informal teaching and learning situations we may find *purposeful* and *incidental* teaching and learning taking place. That is, in both types of situations, the adults may set out purposefully to impart certain knowledge, skills, or attitudes they feel are important for children to understand and accept. On the other hand, much is learned in a teaching situation that is not planned for and in fact may not even be desired. Often incidental learning is more important from the point of view of the learner. The "silent language" of gesture, attitude, and facial expression may modify the behavior far more than the direct act of teaching. As we all know, it is not uncommon for teachers or parents to tell children one thing, but by their tone of voice or by certain actions actually show them that what they say is not what they believe. For example, a teacher may verbally affirm human dignity and worth and at the same time show by his actions that certain groups of people are not "nice" or don't "belong." In such a situation the silent language speaks far louder than the spoken language.

The second point associated with formal and informal education is that in *all* societies both types can be found. The differences between societies in this respect are in the degree of emphasis given to each type. In preindustrial societies very little is taught formally. An illustration is the Hopi Indian culture of the American Southwest. Among the Hopi, it is crucial that the young learn the Hopi way of life. The Hopi are an unaggressive, cooperative people who see their destiny bound to the destiny of the whole universe. The concept of "getting ahead," which plays such a large part in our industrial society, is simply not understandable to them. If one man gets ahead, all get ahead; if one gets behind, all get behind. This way of life must be transmitted to the new generation if the society and its culture is to continue, and almost all of this cultural transmission is informal. The father and mother, aunts and uncles, grandfather and grandmother, through example and admonition, lead the child, step by step, to see the universe from a Hopi point of view.

In contrast to this type of education is the government school which represents the formal aspect of education for Hopi children. In terms of the aims of informal Hopi education, much of what is taught in the government school is not meaningful to these children. The concept of marks and the associated competition to achieve them does not fit the cultural pattern of cooperation and cosmic enterprise which is at the heart of the Hopi culture. In this sense, the government school is destructive of the Hopi culture because it is founded on values which are antithetical to the values of the Hopi society.

In passing, it may be interesting to note that in the United States, where admission to the mainstream of society is based primarily on skin color, much of what is taught to children in the ghettos of large cities in the formal school situation is destructive and not meaningful in terms of the skills necessary for survival. Professional educators have often failed to note that the informal education provided by the peer group, family, and community of the slums is far more real to these children than the "academic" assignments of their teachers. In this sense the subcultures of Negro and Puerto Rican ghettos is preindustrial in character, and it would be wise for educators to recognize this when organizing compensatory educational activities for the so-called "culturally disadvantaged."

Types of Educational Systems

By now the reader may recognize that we are drawing a rather clear-cut dichotomy in terms of preindustrial and industrial societies. This dichotomy is not meant to describe existing societies; it is, rather, an ideational construct which we hope will assist in the understanding of societies and the differences which exist between them as they change from one type to the other.

Similar dichotomies have been presented by social theorists for many years. Perhaps the most famous is the Gemeinschaft–Gesellschaft theory of Ferdinand Tonnies.[2] Related polarizations have been advanced by Redfield, Durkheim, Cooley, Becker, and

[2] Ferdinand Tonnies, *Community and Society*, ed. and trans. Charles P. Loomis (New York: Harper & Row [Harper Torchbooks], 1963), pp. 12–29.

Conflict between the cultural values of a society and those imposed upon it by another society can be seen in the educational situation of the Hopi Indians.

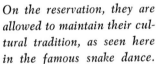

On the reservation, they are allowed to maintain their cultural tradition, as seen here in the famous snake dance.

The children are instructed informally in the tribal religion through the use of their Kachina dolls, which are presented to them in a ceremonial dance.

Yet the children are also required to go to government schools, where the values imparted are alien to the Hopi view of life.

others.[3] The basic premise of these theorists is that certain life
styles, motivations, and moralities, exist in each polar state, i.e.
preindustrial and industrial, and that each produces distinct personalities and particular sets of social relationships. Furthermore
— and this is especially important here — each type of society
tends to accept differing forms of knowledge as valid. In a discussion relating to the matter of knowledge, Tonnies' translator says,

> Gemeinschaft types of society have a traditionally defined fund
> of knowledge handed down as conclusive and final: they are not
> concerned with discovering new ideas or extending their spheres
> of knowledge. Any effort to test traditional knowledge, insofar
> as it implies doubt, is ruled out on moral grounds. In such a
> group, the prevailing methods are ontological and dogmatic;
> . . . In contrast, [the] Gesellschaft) type of organization in-
> stitutionalized techniques for the attainment and codification of
> knowledge. In such a group the methods are primarily epis-
> temological and critical. . . .[4]

If this is the case, and it appears to be, the preindustrial (Gemeinschaft) and the industrial (Gesellschaft) societies must approach
the educational venture in dramatically different ways.

It is important to re-emphasize that these dichotomies are not
descriptions but actually theoretical models which can be used to
examine existing societies.

In a similar manner, the theoretical models of educational systems that are about to be proposed are not actual descriptions of
existing educational systems. They too are conceptual models
with which to examine educational change in a varying cultural
milieu. If we can keep this fact in mind and refrain from attempting to fit these models to existing educational systems, much
confusion will be avoided.

It is possible to identify three types of educational systems, any
of which theoretically could be found in whole or in part at any
time and in any geographical location. It is important to note
that two of these systems correspond to the gemeinschaft–gesellschaft types of society discussed above.

---

[3] Tonnies, *loc. cit.*
[4] Tonnies, *loc. cit.*, p. 28.

The Conservative System

The first of these is the *conservative* system of education. As the term implies, the basic goal of this type of educational system is to preserve the heritage of the past and to transmit it to the next generation much as it was received. This system emphasizes the transmission aspect of education and utilizes informal teaching–learning to accomplish this end. This type of education is generally found in folk–rural–preindustrial societies. The basic objective is to preserve the status quo or at least to guard against radical innovations. For the most part, such societies are based on agreed-upon patterns of acceptable behavior that are frequently founded on, or at least supported by, the religious traditions of the past, and educational energies are spent in insuring cultural continuity.

The Progressive System

As these societies enter into an industrial or technological phase, however, the emphasis on conservation begins to break down. Increasingly, as a result of urbanization and the increase in alternative points of view, it becomes difficult for education to remain primarily oriented to cultural induction or to remain informal. As the tempo of industrialization accelerates, there is a corresponding development of special skills and occupations. Formal education must develop at a rate necessary to supply the demands of the occupational market. Teachers become more specialized as well as do the types of schools in which the teaching is done.

In such a dynamic societal and cultural milieu, the mere passing on of the cultural heritage is difficult if not impossible. First of all, it becomes extremely difficult to isolate those aspects of the culture which all people need, and second, the speed with which changes take place requires new and unique institutions with which to meet the needs of the society. Such widespread change requires the development of a second type of educational system which we may call the *progressive* system. This system of education is devoted to the development of critical skills for the evaluation of old institutions and the creation of new ones that are relevant to the new circumstances. It also tends to stress the use of the scientific method as a means of expanding knowledge.

THE RADICAL SYSTEM

A third category of educational system — but one which is outside the preindustrial–industrial continuum — is that which has been called *radical*. A radical school system is one which is in the control of an intellectual, political, or economic elite dedicated to the establishment of a radically different social order. Such a school system is founded on the principles of indoctrination and imposition. Its major task is to establish and perpetuate a preconceived notion of an ideal state.

It is a basic democratic principle that man must be assisted in developing the skill and the will to dissent and innovate or the democratic ideal will be lost before it is realized. Thus, the radical system is undemocratic. Although it is possible to have a benevolent elite who will make decisions in terms of what is "good" for the rest of mankind, the danger of corruptive power is far too great to warrant such a risk. Radical educational systems, however efficient they may be, tend to raise up the state as its god, and man — for whom the state was originally designed — becomes its slave.

Elements of radicalism exist in many educational systems which in themselves are conservative or progressive, but on the whole these elements are not significant enough to categorize the whole system as radical.

Each of these types of educational systems are expressions of the power of decision making groups to perpetuate or modify the existing culture in terms of their own values. In the following discussion, "values" and "culture" will be equated, even though philosophically some considerable distinctions could be made. Both of these terms will be used to refer to the configurations of cultural items which are held by a society to be desirable and worth perpetuating.

Ideal and Actual Cultures

THE CULTURE GAP

It can be said that all societies have both an ideal and an actual culture. That is, all societies have a level of culture that expresses the "highest" or most desirable goals of the people. This is the "ought" level of human behavior, attitudes, artifacts, etc. Such aphorisms or beliefs as "Honesty is the best policy," "the state may not interfere with freedom of speech," "children ought to respect their parents," are all examples of *ideal* goals of American culture. But even though most of us may agree on certain ideal types of behavior, frequently we do not behave in these ways at all, and this behavior is termed the *actual* level of culture. This does not always mean that we are hypocritical; it may merely suggest that our goals have become unreal or outmoded. This disparity between ideal and actual levels of culture is called (somewhat unimaginatively) the *culture gap.*

In all societies, the role of education, either formal or informal, is to close the culture gap or to assist people to reach the ideal goals of the society. Among people where there is almost universal agreement on what these goals are, both formal and informal educative efforts will be used to reinforce each other. In societies in which this agreement does not exist, formal and informal education often will be in conflict. It is not difficult to find circumstances in which the family or peer group is not sympathetic to the efforts or goals of the school. Frequently the language patterns used in schools are not at all the "real" language of life. Although children may be careful not to say "I ain't got no money" while in school, they may not hesitate to use ungrammatical expressions outside the schoolroom. This picture of conflict between the school's concept of societal goals and the society at large may be extended when one begins to examine the wide range of expressed goals in a pluralistic society.

CULTURAL LAG

In a significant work on social change written in 1922, William Fielding Ogburn introduced the concept of *cultural lag.*[5] It was Ogburn's thesis that cultural elements could be classified as material or non-material (adaptive). His hypothesis was that these elements of the culture tended to change at varying rates and that in the unevenness of change certain maladjustments resulted. As an example, we might cite the invention of the automobile in the early years of this century. Until this time the horse was considered the ideal means of transporting people and goods from

[5] William F. Ogburn, *Social Change* (New York: Viking Press, 1922), p. 200.

India's famine problem is a result of overpopulation due to a cultural lag between birth control concepts and practices.

one place to another, and many people wondered who the crack-pots were who piloted the funny-looking, smelly, noisy "auto" down the street frightening horses and children. Did they really think that such a contraption would ever be seriously used by sane people? A great deal of effort was required before the adaptive or non-material cultures could accommodate the ever-increasing use of the automobile. In other words, for a considerable period a cultural lag existed between the automobile as a technological, material part of the culture and the non-material adaptive aspects of the culture which were required to deal with it.

Considerable criticism has been leveled against Ogburn's theory, useful though it has been. One such criticism is that if the technological advance is based on a value which is held by the people, no cultural lag results. An example of this is the preservation of food by refrigeration. For decades ice was the only known means of keeping certain foods cold enough to prevent spoilage, but with the development of the electric refrigerator the ice box was quickly abandoned by all those who could afford the new equipment. No serious cultural lag ensued with the introduction of refrigeration because the basic value associated with pure and unspoiled food was held by most of the people. On the other hand, the development of contraceptive devices as a means of controlling the population has introduced considerable cultural lag because it is based on a cultural value which is *not* held by all people.

We may also cite two examples of cultural lag in the field of education. The introduction of educational television into American schools at first caused a great deal of anxiety among teachers, who felt that the personal relationship between teacher and pupil was being threatened. Similarly, the use of teaching machines has been resisted because of the "conditioned" quality of the teaching–learning process implied by this innovation. In each instance, had the technological advance been interpreted as a means of achieving a desired end more effectively, little cultural lag would have occurred.

Cultural lag also may be seen in the difficulty of communication between certain segments of the society. Frequently teenagers take on, as perfectly normal, patterns of behavior brought about by the advance of technology which are rejected by the older members of society. A case in point is the use of hallucinogenic drugs, which are finding increasing use by young adults, despite the dire warnings by their elders that the drugs may cause serious physical and mental injury. Another example is the growing opulence and related consumption patterns of teenagers resulting from our expanding economy. Those of us who lived through the Depression and World War II feel somehow uneasy when we see the buy-now-pay-later philosophy becoming so common among youth. It is not unusual for two generations to be out of communication — indeed, it has always been so — but with change occurring so rapidly in our time the problem of cultural lag between generations becomes increasingly significant.

Education and Cultural Change

AN ANALYSIS OF CULTURE

A useful tool in understanding cultures and cultural change is that developed by anthropologist Ralph Linton in his book, *The Study of Man*.[6] Linton theorized that cultures are made up of elements which could be classified as *universals, specialties,* and

---

[6] Ralph Linton, *The Study of Man* (New York: Appleton-Century-Crofts, 1936), pp. 271–287.

alternatives. Universals are those cultural elements which are held as valuable and worthy of perpetuating from one generation to another. An example of a universal in American culture is the belief in some supernatural power. Even though there may be large numbers of people who do not hold this to be true, the normative position with respect to God is that He does exist. The belief in God then would be a universal.

Specialties are those cultural elements which are seen as valuable or whose product is seen as valuable, but which are not understood by the majority of societal members. As the name implies, the cultural element or specialty is known to a select group of people but not to the total population, even though most of the members of society see the perpetuation of this element as desirable. Such a cultural element might relate to law, medicine, or conservation. We seek out the services of lawyers when we have need for them, and even though their knowledge is unknown to us we generally abide by the advice they give. We, in effect, value the product of their knowledge. It would take little thought to identify the literally hundreds and hundreds of specialties existing in present-day American culture.

The third category is that of alternatives. Cultural elements which fall into this category are those that are in conflict. That is, groups of people hold conflicting views regarding the worth of a particular pattern of behavior, attitude, artifact, etc.

If one were to examine a list of cultural elements making up the total culture and could classify the items into one of the above groups one would get some idea of the degree of integration of the society. The greater the number of elements classified as universals, the greater would be the cohesiveness of the people; conversely, the greater the number of alternatives to be found, the less the cohesiveness or the greater the disintegration. If we were to draw a diagram of the former type of society, it might look something like this:

In the culture represented, all children would learn the same things, discounting the division of labor by sex. In this kind of society education is relatively easy. The models are clear and directly presented and all segments of the society would reinforce the skills and knowledge to be transmitted. Here is the Gemeinschaft, or preindustrial society in action.

Now let us turn to a diagram representing an industrialized society or Gesellschaft:

Here, the society is in little general agreement about what is to be taught to all children. The "core" of universals is small in comparison to the specialties and alternatives. The society is technologically advanced and provides a wide range of occupations and specialties to its young. The great number of alternatives present indicates the disunity of the society. Imitation of model behavior is extremely difficult. A child may in his early years take as desirable behavior that of his parents and grandparents, but almost immediately upon venturing outside his home, he meets with tremendous variation in what is considered acceptable behavior. (Although it is true that housing patterns of large urban areas do tend to segregate life styles to some degree, the over-all effect of the ghetto or middle class suburb is not significant in terms of *developing* standardized behavior. Within a one- or two-block area in a large urban ghetto one may expect to find relatively wide differences in occupations, attitudes, and tastes. It is for this reason that the term "Negro culture" is for all practical purposes meaningless. Economic circumstance does, to a considerable extent, standardize behavior, but its effect on personality differences is far less than is usually imagined.)

In societies in which such a wide range of alternatives exists, a child cannot expect a consistent model of what is appropriate father behavior, or mother behavior, or even religious behavior. Lacking such models, he is increasingly required to make judgments for himself. Education in such societies, then, must be progressive, in the context in which this term has been used previously in this chapter. Also, because of the great variety of specialties available, education becomes increasingly formal. With technological development comes knowledge expansion and vice versa. In each area of specialization a greater and greater body of facts, techniques, and even language develops, which those outside the specialty can never hope to know. As a consequence children begin to specialize at an ever earlier age. It is true that those within the formal educative structure attempt to identify commonly needed skills and knowledge, but the logic which supports their decisions comes increasingly under attack by those who are at variance with it. It is in such circumstances that the significance of pressure groups or vested interest groups can be seen. Each group, having selected a portion of the total culture as having relevance for all members of the society, attempts to bring pressure legitimately or illegitimately upon the school to get its interests represented in the curriculum. Admittedly this is democratic and necessary, but it poses continual and serious curricular problems for school personnel.

Education in an industrial society must, then, by the nature of the culture, become increasingly process-oriented. Obviously, subject matter content will be of great significance, but this content will consist less and less of elements of the common culture; rather, it will consist of those skills, facts, and attitudes which are seen as relevant to a particular specialty. It is quite possible in the future that industries, service agencies, and other institutions will develop their own schools to provide effective and efficient education for those entering their specialties. To summarize this point, then, it can be said that the structure of a school as well as the techniques, methods, and curriculum will, to a considerable extent, reflect the values of a society as well as the degree of cohesiveness of its people.

A STRUCTURAL SCHEMA OF EDUCATION

In theory, the formal and informal institutions of education should possess an internal consistency between the goals of the system (values) and the methods, materials, and curriculum used to achieve these goals. Figure 1, which is relevant to either pre-

industrial or industrial societies, shows the relationships between
the subparts of the educational process and the total institution.
As this diagram shows, societal values ought to be reflected in the
aims of education. Obviously, if the group holding power or
making the most crucial societal decisions intends to achieve its
goals, the educational system must support these goals. Thus, a
society which believes in the dignity and worth of the individual
would have in its statement of aims each child's development of
a self-concept of dignity and worth. The materials, methods, and
curriculum, as well as the organizational structure of the system

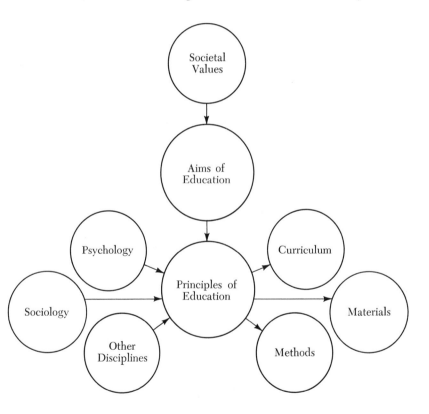

FIGURE 1

The Educational Process

itself, should also reflect this goal. And the principles of education which derive from the knowledge gained in the parent disciplines of psychology, sociology, anthropology, biology, and others should be consistent with the aims and values of the school system and the group in power. If, for example, a society believed man to be a rational and choosing animal whose destiny is achieved through self-direction, it is inconceivable that teachers and administrators would support or tolerate educational methods which reflected the view that all human behavior may be explained through conditioned response. If such were the case, considerable conflict would result, and the professional life of any teacher whose basic values showed such variance from the values of the system would be one of frustration, anxiety, or duplicity.

It may be inferred, then, from Figure 1, that educational systems should be articulated totalities. The fact is, however, that the educational systems of all but the most primitive societies lack such articulation (and we use the word "primitive" advisedly because few societies are really primitive, regardless of their stage of technological development). As has been indicated earlier, the culture of all groups is in constant change, and almost all change brings about some lack of communication between segments of the society.

All of this brings us at last to the process of educational change in general and in American education in particular. There is no attempt here to be exhaustive in terms of all of the factors which bring about change in education, but the principles presented would appear to be important ones and useful for understanding the conflicts in present-day American education.

EDUCATIONAL CHANGE

The polar positions of Gemeinschaft and Gesellschaft or (preindustrial and industrial societies) coincide with informal and formal education and with conservative and progressive education. Furthermore, the analytical scheme of Linton (universals, specialties, and alternatives) in terms of the proportion of cultural items assigned to each, can also be used to clarify the significance of the continuum as it is applied to education. It will also be advisable to recall the bivalent definition of education introduced at the beginning of this chapter — that education is the process by which the child is inducted into the culture as well as the process by which the young are assisted in developing the skills of critical appraisal. If we can keep these factors in mind, the remarks which follow should have greater meaning.

Educational change is to a considerable extent the result of cultural change, whether it comes about through the relatively slow process of cultural evolution or the sudden upheaval of revolution. The interplay of newly accepted values and the development and embracing of new knowledge has profound effect on cultures and, as a consequence, on education. In discussing the rise of progressive education in his significant book, *The Transformation of the School,* Lawrence Cremin says,

> . . . progressive education began as a vast humanitarian effort to apply the promise of American life — the ideal government by, of, and for the people — to the puzzling new urban–industrial civilization that came into being during the latter half of the nineteenth century. The word *progressive* provides the clue to what it really was: the educational phases of American Progressivism writ large.[7]

Cremin adds that a totally new view of what man might become was developing. Institutions, ideas, artifacts — indeed the whole value structure — was being altered, and as such the school simply reflected this change. We do not intend to suggest here that American schools changed overnight — in fact, to a considerable extent, they still have not changed significantly — but the changes which did and are occurring have been more a reflection of the increasing acceptance of a new way of life and the growing body of knowledge supporting this life style than of the ideas of a single person or group.

This theory does not explain all educational change, however, in spite of the ample evidence which supports it. The quick and decisive political coups which have occurred in the past and which continue to occur in various parts of the world attest to the fact that educational change is also the result of shifts in political power. Though it is not always true that educational change comes about when a new power-holding group takes the political

[7] Lawrence Cremin, *The Transformation of the School* (New York: Alfred A. Knopf, 1961), p. viii.

reins of a country, it is almost patent to say that if the educational system did not support the radically different value system of the new leaders, the new regime would not last long. Such dramatic change can be seen in the revolutionary innovations in education that went into effect soon after the Bolshevik revolution in Russia in 1917 and in those that occurred in Communist China after 1949. In terms of the types of educational systems discussed earlier in this chapter it is quite clear that these systems must be called radical.

AMERICAN EDUCATION TODAY

We have attempted to develop a theoretical framework by which educational change can be interpreted in any time or geographical circumstance, including present-day American society. The thesis has been that as countries move from a preindustrial society to an industrial society the educational emphasis must shift from informal to formal practices. Therefore, the type of education possible and even necessary in the old agrarian American culture can no longer be useful in the industrial society of the late twentieth century. Yet we believe that, to a considerable extent, the United States has retained the fundamental structure, methods, materials, and curriculum of a period which has passed. Moreover, our pluralistic society cannot agree upon what the schools ought to teach, and yet the schools continue to operate as if they had a particular charge from the society as a whole. If there ever was a consistency between the aims of American education and the methods, materials, and curriculum used, there is ample evidence that we do not have it now.

The growing impatience with educational practices at almost every level is evidence of the inarticulation which exists between the young and the adult segments of the society as well as between professional educators and the lay population. Admittedly the problem is complex and no easy solution is at hand, but as we stated in the beginning of this chapter, we must at least concede that man is a rational animal and that as such he should be able to utilize the knowledge he possesses to solve present and future problems. In terms of his educational future and the future of his total culture, he cannot say "Que será, será, Whatever will be, will be."

SUGGESTIONS FOR FURTHER READING

Biesanz, John, and Mavis Biesanz. *Modern Society: An Introduction to Social Change,* 3rd ed. Englewood Cliffs, N.J.: Prentice-Hall, 1964.

Hodgkinson, Harold L. *Education in Social and Cultural Perspectives.* Englewood Cliffs, N.J.: Prentice-Hall, 1962.

McLendon, Jonathon C. *Social Foundations of Education.* New York: The Macmillan Co., 1966.

Mulhern, James A. *A History of Education: A Social Interpretation.* New York: The Ronald Press Company, 1959.

Pounds, Ralph L., and James R. Bryner. *The School in American Society.* New York: The Macmillan Co., 1967.

Riesman, David. *The Lonely Crowd.* New Haven, Conn.: Yale University Press, 1961.

Shapiro, Harry L. (ed.). *Man, Culture, and Society.* New York: Oxford University Press, 1960.

Spindler, George D. (ed.). *Education and Culture: Anthropological Approaches.* New York: Holt, Rinehart & Winston, 1963.

The American city has been the scene of rapid
social change for some time.

Chapter Four

SOCIALIZATION
AND CULTURAL CHANGE

Socialization

Socialization is in many ways a frightening word. For some, it carries the gray tones of an Orwellian collectivistic society. For others, it calls to mind a world of teas and dances and white gloves. From one point of view or another, the word seems to imply a set of rules and restrictions — "you must do this" or "you must not do that."

Modern social theorists, however, use the term in a much wider sense. To cultural anthropologists, it means the process by which one takes on a pattern of behavior that is of value to a particular social group. In other words, the socialization process is the way one becomes "human" as defined in a particular cultural setting. Admittedly, using such a definition involves considerable risk, because it immediately raises the question, What is human nature? Do all men have a common nature, or are we totally the product of our particular experience? This is the old nature-nurture controversy which, though it should have been buried long ago, is still raised.

For our purposes here, however, socialization may be defined as the transactional process by which the biological potential of a person becomes realized within a particular environmental setting. If this definition seems almost as frightening as the ones above, it need not be. What it means is simply that the potentialities of human beings are realized or developed in an environment which is hospitable to them. For example, a person with the potential to be a pianist could never be one in a world without a piano. We may carry this idea even further to say that despite the commonly held conception of heredity that a father and mother with blue eyes will produce blue-eyed children, the fact is that unless environmental conditions are hospitable to blue eyes, no blue eyes will appear. This is tantamount to saying that what we have, we have because the conditions necessary for producing what we have were present. Gardner Murphy has even gone so far as to say that the difference between men and birch trees is the difference in the quality of response of the biochemical structure of the two to a common environmental circumstance.[1]

Although this concept may appear to be obscure, it is simply another way of saying that what any living thing is, is the result of the transaction between its biological potential and its environment. For some, it provides an exciting explanation for the vast range of unique characteristics that are found among all plants and animals. It helps us understand the individual personalities in a group of sparrows at the bird feeder or the aggressive and unaggressive nature of puppies in a litter, or the loving, open, empathetic person as compared to one who is hostile, narrow, and unforgiving.

Socialization, then, is the transactional process by which the biological potential of an individual is realized in a particular environmental setting. It is necessary, however, to keep in mind that neither the potentiality of man nor the environment in which he exists is constant. The very transaction which takes place alters the potentiality as well as the environment. Obviously, this is not a new concept. In the sixth century A.D., Heraclitus, in speaking of the constant flux of life, said that no man could put his foot into the same river twice. Approximately fourteen cen-

[1] Gardner Murphy, *Personality* (New York: Harper & Brothers, 1947), p. 53.

turies later, John Dewey, in discussing habit, made substantially the same point:

> The basic characteristic of habit is that every experience enacted and undergone modifies the one who acts and undergoes, while this modification affects, whether we wish it or not, the quality of subsequent experience. . . .
>
> Experience does not go on simply inside a person. It goes on there, for it influences the formation of attitudes of desire and purpose. But this is not the whole story. Every genuine experience has an active side which changes in some degree the objective conditions under which experiences are had.[2]

Extending the concept of transaction, Alan Watts, in an address on Zen Buddhism in 1964, said that man is not only the product of the transaction between his nature and the nature of the external world but also is, in the Zen image, both in and of his environment and even *is* his environment.[3]

From the foregoing it should be clear that socialization is a reciprocal process in which the organism is continually being altered by and altering the environment. This concept is a far cry from the unsophisticated notion of conditioning, of stimulus–response, or something being done to a person by external forces. It is a natural, person-engaging, living process. No individual born into a society can avoid the transaction of socialization.

Despite the necessity of defining the process of becoming human in a social context, the total process cannot be comprehended without understanding the significance of non-human circumstances in the environment as well. Events, ideas, and geography all can be significant factors in shaping the growth of human personality. One need only visit the ghettos in large urban centers, with their squalor, drabness, and rotting buildings infested with rats and bugs to recognize that significant non-human factors are continually operating to produce the hopelessness and frustration of many of the residents. Therefore, to dismiss the non-human factor in the process of socialization is to eliminate a fundamental part of personality development. To return to Gardner Mur-

---

[2] John Dewey, *Experience and Education* (New York: Collier Books, 1963), p. 35.

[3] Tape of informal address given by Allan Watts at the University of Wisconsin-Milwaukee, 1964.

phy's comparison of men and birch trees, men are men because of the quality of their response to the environment, and the environment includes far more than just other men.

We must pause here to clarify one or two of the ideas presented thus far. In the foregoing pages, we have attempted a definition of man which is essentially biosocial. To accept this definition of man as a biosocial organism, however, is not to say that man might not be defined according to other important points of view. He has been and probably will continue to be defined from a psychological, biological, and spiritual point of view, and in such definitions we see no conflict with the position taken here. Man is many things, and with the knowledge we have about him at present, we can only say with certainty what we think he is not. We have not come to any lasting conclusions regarding what he is.

The second point of clarification is that we have been talking about man in a very generic sense, that is, as a member of the species homo sapiens. To end here is to account only for his general response to the environment in the sense that he can be defined in a common and general way according to common and general criteria. What is significant, however, is not man's response in a general sense, but the specific individual response of one's unique biological potential. Therefore, the definition of all human behavior, in the last analysis, is that it is the unique growth, development, and reaction patterns of specific individuals.

The definition of socialization presented above also introduces several concepts which need further clarification as we proceed with the discussion of socialization in a changing society.

SIGNIFICANT SYMBOLS

The concept "significant symbol" was introduced in the work of George Herbert Mead, a noted social psychologist who taught at the University of Chicago during the first three decades of this century. Mead used the term in connection with communication, as follows:

> The importance of what we term communication lies in the fact that it provides a form of behavior in which the organism or the individual may become an object of himself. It is that sort of communication which we have been discussing — not

communication in the sense of the cluck of the hen to the chickens, or the bark of the wolf to the pack, or the lowing of a cow, but communication in the sense of *significant symbols* [italics ours], communication which is directed not only to others but also to the individual himself. So far as that type of communication is a part of behavior it at least introduces a self. Of course one may hear without listening; one may see things that he does not realize; do things that he is not really aware of. But it is where one does respond to that which he addresses to another and where that response of his own becomes a part of his conduct, where he not only hears himself but responds to himself, talks and replies to himself as truly as the other person replies to him, that we have behavior in which the individuals become objects to themselves.[4]

What Mead is saying is that true communication exists when we know that what we say has the same meaning for others as it has for us. He is also suggesting that such communication is possible only when we learn the significance of such symbols in a social milieu. Unless we have internalized the attitudes, mores, and expectations of the social group in which we live, we can never really develop ourselves and therefore never really communicate. The interesting point in all of this is that the growth in the ability to communicate with others can be interpreted as the growth of self. If the dialogue with other persons is at the same time a dialogue with ourselves, we must gradually be developing into a self among selves. In short, we are becoming persons.

STATUS POSITION

Perhaps the use of another set of concepts will assist us in this discussion. The term "status position" is one which has been used by sociologists for a long time, but it might be helpful to review it here. A status position is said to be a position occupied by an individual in a particular society. It is also a position which can be arranged within a hierarchy of other status positions in the society, from superior to inferior. That is, we assign various levels of prestige to various status positions — some higher, others lower, on a continuum from high to low. For example, the position of

[4] Anselm Strauss (ed.), *The Social Psychology of George Herbert Mead* (Chicago: University of Chicago Press, 1956), p. 215.

President of the United States is a status position to which the highest prestige is given, while the position of street cleaner is one of very low prestige. It is important to say, however, that we are talking about the position in the abstract and not specific individuals who occupy such positions, although, admittedly, it is often difficult to make such a separation. In societies which are relatively stable (changing slowly), the same status positions tend to remain necessary to the functioning of the society generation after generation, with much the same degree of prestige assigned to them. In such societies few new status positions develop, nor is it likely that existing ones are abandoned easily. However, if some radical innovation in technology is introduced, marked changes in life style involving status positions may occur. An interesting account of such sweeping change can be found in Ralph Linton's *The Study of Man*.[5]

The Tanala were hill people occupying a part of Western Madagascar. For centuries they had cleared the forests to grow rice, using a dry rice farming technique. The cleared land was divided jointly among the families in accordance with the land's ability to produce a crop sufficient to meet the requirements of the joint family, and the produce of the joint effort was divided among the households according to their needs. The total society was built upon a communal–democratic concept of shared purposes and needs.

Wet rice cultivation techniques first appeared as a casual addition to the dry rice farming patterns, but soon it became apparent that planting on wet ground was superior to planting on dry ground in terms of the amount of rice produced. Families which had been used to moving when the fertility of the land was exhausted were unwilling to leave when the wet rice farming techniques produced heavy harvests year after year. Gradually there came into being a land-holding group which was able to accumulate a surplus of rice far beyond family needs. Such a surplus constituted power and wealth, and it is not difficult to understand the leap which was taken to declare the family with the most power and wealth as divinely sanctioned. With this self-proclaimed investiture a kingship was established, and the old Tanala pattern of existence was almost completely obliterated.

[5] Ralph Linton, *The Study of Man* (New York: Appleton-Century-Crofts, 1936), p. 189.

The introduction of wet rice farming techniques into a life style built almost wholly on dry rice farming changed the culture so drastically that for all practical purposes the Tanala culture as it had been known disappeared. Where the social organization had been communal and democratic, it became a monarchy. Where land was held along joint family lines, the concept of individual land tenure developed. Although it would be interesting to examine other basic changes in the culture which occurred as a result of this innovation, the important point for this discussion is that with these changes dramatic alterations come about in the status positions traditionally held by the Tanala. Where no absolute ruler had existed, the position of king developed, with all the prestige and power normally assigned. Where once the village elders had the power to distribute property and solve the problems of the people, with the new patterns of agriculture and land tenure they lost their position as arbiters and judges. It is presumed that other status positions among the Tanala were altered as well.

The illustration of change in status among the Tanala is a simple example of the much more rapid and continual change occurring in status positions in societies which are highly technological. Exploding knowledge, with the associated development of new industries, the ecumenical movement in established churches, the change from a production-oriented economy to a service-oriented economy must all combine to introduce status positions never known before and to alter those in existence, as well as to cause the abandonment of positions held in high esteem in the past.

ROLE

"Role" is the dynamic aspect of status. That is, it is the set of expected behaviors associated with a particular status position, and an individual occupying a status position should understand the agreed-upon actions, dress, and speech patterns which have been built around that position. Indeed, frequently if one occupying a status position does not act in the manner expected, he is punished or removed from that status. In the army, for example, when one is accused of "conduct unbecoming an officer," the accusation is precisely aimed at the officer's not behaving as his status demands or, rather, as the army expects an officer to be-have.

When a person is acting in terms of his status position, his posi-tion should be identifiable by his style of behavior. Obviously, the narrower the range of possible behaviors associated with a status, and the more particularistic that behavior — that is, the more precise each behavior is — the easier it will be to identify the status position being occupied. For example, if the king were the only person who could ride in a gold limousine, and further, if he were not allowed to ride in any other kind of a vehicle, then if we saw someone riding in a gold limousine we would expect it to be the king. We would have been able to identify the position by the associated behavior. If, on the other hand, the king and several of his officials could all ride in gold limousines, or if they could all ride in several different vehicles painted any of a num-ber of different colors, it would become increasingly difficult, if not impossible, to identify the status position of the occupants. Flags, crests, and uniforms have historically been used to assist in the identification of status. Again, in societies where status positions have fairly narrow and particularistic roles, it is fairly easy to identify and to learn both status and the associated role. As will be seen later, the learning of status and role is an im-portant part of the socialization process.

GENERALIZED OTHER

Now let us return to George Herbert Mead's point that a dia-logue with one's self as well as with others is necessary for per-sonality development. Mead also believed that the process of becoming a self is the process of internalizing the expectations, attitudes, or roles of all the others in his social setting, and that this involves learning the roles others are expected to play, but also one's own role behavior. In this internalization process, Mead says, the roles of these various societal members become general-ized and organized into a total social view which he terms a "generalized other."[6]

The importance of this generalized other for our discussion be-comes clear when we realize that in societies which are relatively

[6] Strauss, *op. cit.*, p. 86.

static or changing slowly role and status positions change slowly as well. Thus, in this kind of society, the process of learning the attitudes and roles of others and internalizing them as a generalized other is relatively easy. Although it is true that the generalized other is never fixed — i.e., the attitudinal postures of all individuals in a society are constantly changing, if only because of continuous experience — still the social structure is so clearly established that the changes which occur can be planned for and accommodated. In most societies, "rites of passage" are built into the culture to allow for maturation and the assumption of new roles and status.

Now if we translate this process of a developing generalized other into a society whose culture is in rapid transition and where new status positions and roles are introduced almost daily while old ones are disappearing, and further, where the status positions which have existed in the past are being redefined continually, one begins to appreciate both the difficulty of communication and the severity of the problem of self-identification. This difficulty of communication and self-identification is closely related to the growing phenomenon of alienation, a concept which is currently receiving much attention and discussion in the United States and which will be considered here in Chapter Five.

THE SECURITY SYSTEM

Associated with the concepts of status, role, and generalized other is that which has been termed the "security system." In this sense, the security system is that configuration of proved patterns of relationships which have been developed by an individual to enable him to live successfully with the external world. Here again, though the social milieu is fundamental to human survival, any security system must provide for successful relationships with the non-human world as well.

From birth — although there is considerable evidence to indicate that the process begins much earlier — the human organism begins its exploration of the environment into which it is born. To a considerable extent, such initial probing is the means by which one's basic physiological needs are satisfied. Admittedly, much of this exploration is through trial and error, but it is not long after birth that the "appropriate" ways of satisfying such needs begin to be impressed upon the child through a kind of conditioning process imposed by the parents. Later the range of conditioning agents is increased to other significant humans in the child's environment, and ideally, as time goes on, the total range of human needs are met through the security system.

The patterns of eating, eliminating waste, and even play have socially sanctioned rules which are considered necessary by adults. These are the social norms, or "rules of the game." When such rules are clear and specific and constant within a developmental period (for example, within early childhood as opposed to adolescence), the building of an adequate security system is relatively easy. In other words, in societies which are extremely homogeneous in terms of their cultures — where most people agree upon certain specified ways of accomplishing societal goals — the children in all families will be treated in much the same way. They will be taught the same songs and stories, they will learn to eat the same food, their clothes will be cut in the same fashion and worn in the same manner, and they will be punished for the same acts in the same ways. That is, the total society has approved of the same social norms. No matter where the child is in the community, he will be expected to behave as his parents expect him to behave. Thus, all the conditioning agents will tend to reinforce the establishment of the security system. In such societies it is possible to speak of a "way of life" and be fairly certain that all those who participate will know and approve of what is meant.

But if the ways in which need satisfaction is realized are various and changing within a short time, or if the other conditioning agents in the child's life accept these differing ways as appropriate to such need satisfaction, the development of an adequate and functioning security system is difficult and confusing.

The Changing American Society

CULTURAL VARIATION

Man has produced a wide range of cultural forms by which he has attempted to solve his problems. So varied and diverse have these cultural forms been from historical period to historical period and from geographic location to geographic location that it is almost impossible to comprehend. We in the stream of Western civilization, who support many of our beliefs and values by the Judaic-Christian tradition, find it extremely difficult to understand how such practices as the premarital sexual experiences of the Samoan girl can have societal approval or on what basis the ill will and treachery of the Dobu can be sanctioned, let alone prized. Those within a particular tradition tend to look upon all ways of life which are different from one's own as quaint, exotic, and even "uncivilized." We readily apply the word "primitive" to those societies which have not built a vast technological or industrial culture without realizing that most cultures are highly complex and even sophisticated, though the values upon which those cultures are built are not those upon which our society is based.

Ruth Benedict, in one of the classic writings in the field of anthropology, has said,

> In culture . . . we must imagine a great arc on which are ranged the possible interests provided either by the human age-cycle or by the environment or by man's various activities. A culture that capitalized even a considerable proportion of these would be as unintelligible as a language that used all the clicks, all the glottal stops, all the labials, dentals, sibilants, and gutterals from voiceless to voiced and from oral to nasal. Its identity as a culture depends upon the selection of some segments of this arc. Every human society everywhere has made such selection in its cultural institutions.[7]

What Benedict is saying is that factors of history, environment, and just plain human imagination are responsible for the selection of particular ways of behaving over others, and that the selection is not necessarily based on reason. Indeed, the possibility of choosing one style of behavior over another on a rational basis may be eliminated altogether by virtue of the religious traditions held by the society. The use of birth control devices may be used as a case in point. In societies in which religious teaching against the use of artificial means of population control exists, one can anticipate large families, and, in fact, even societal approval of large families as evidence of the fulfillment of one's obligations to the deity.

[7] Ruth Benedict, *Patterns of Culture* (New York: Mentor Books, 1934), p. 21.

The factors of lack of food and extreme human congestion in restricted land areas are not seen as sufficient evidence to reverse
the trend. Empirical evidence in this situation is just not enough.

Of course, this is not to say that forces of reason have not
pressed heavily for cultural modification. The response of the
Spartans to their unique relationship with the helots is a case in
point. Lycurgus, in his zealousness to restore the Dorian military
might, made a conscious and basically successful attempt to establish a military state which struck ultimately at every existing institution within Spartan society.

Although divergence and variation in cultural patterns is a
question of great complexity which cannot be explained easily, it
is nevertheless of tremendous significance in any discussion of
socialization. The cultural milieu in which an individual is raised
is fundamental to the life view with which he perceives his world.
His ability to explain himself to himself as well as to the world
is inextricably bound to his cultural envelope, and those seeking
to understand others must take this factor into significant account.

Cultural Pluralism in America

The civilization which we call America has been from the beginning diverse and pluralistic. Almost from the time of the settlement of Jamestown and Plymouth, men and women of widely
different backgrounds and stations lived and worked to establish
the new nation, and with the growing immigration from all over
Europe, Asia, and Africa the cultural complexity has increased.

Despite the glowing rhetoric of Fourth of July orators, America
has never been a "melting pot." Although it is true that the public
schools have assisted the many and varied peoples who have come
to the United States in becoming citizens, it has never succeeded
in causing these groups to abandon their rich cultures to any significant degree. For example, one can still identify in large urban
centers cultural islands of Irish, Italians, Puerto Ricans, and
Poles. And if one were to look at the country as a whole, one
could locate large groups of Finnish and Cornish in Upper Michigan and Wisconsin, Mexicans in the Southwest, Germans in Wisconsin, Missouri, and Pennsylvania, and Hollanders in lower
Michigan. These people are all loyal Americans to be sure, but
they have retained the flavor of their cultural heritage, and though

Boston's North End is the center of a large Italian community which preserves its ethnic ways. The entire city makes use of the well known outdoor market.

Pennsylvania's Amish are another group who have maintained their own culture. The dress of these young children reflects the non-materialistic and simplistic values held by the Amish, values unchanged by the influence of the rest of contemporary America.

in earlier times many of them tried to mask their ethnic origins by name changes, at present there appears to be a resurgence of pride in one's national heritage.

In another vein, quite apart from nationality or race except in the case of Negroes and Spanish-speaking Americans, this country has been divided along class lines from the very beginning of its history. For the most part, this class structure has been based on economics. The classic work of Warner and Lunt[8] describes the inequality of "life chances" available to Americans on the basis of their membership in one or another social class.

An integral part of the concept of life chances is the assumption that individuals in specific classes behave in ways which identify them as members of that class. Expressions such as "He is being typically middle class" or "They behave exactly as the lower class behaves" are quite common. However, although this concept has been extremely useful, recent research seems to indicate that neither the categories of class as such nor the associated behavior patterns are as discrete as has been previously assumed. The differences between the actual population of the United States and that upon which the study by Warner and Lunt was based are apparently so great that it is impossible to infer the findings of this research of twenty-six years ago to the total population.

But in spite of this criticism of the Warner and Lunt study, the fact remains that people do live differently from one another in some kind of consistent pattern. Furthermore, all status studies suggest that there is a commonality of behavior among certain groups of people (classes), even though much of this behavior is shared by others in other groups. The significance of all of this for us is that an individual raised in a certain life style will perceive himself in a particular way that will be both unique to him but will also be shared to some extent by his close associates.

Another factor which has, until relatively recent times, tended to cause and perpetuate value differences among Americans is the geographical distribution of the people. The traditions associated with the part of the country in which a particular group

[8] W. Lloyd Warner and Paul S. Lunt, *The Social Life of a Modern Community* (New Haven: Yale University Press, 1941).

lives are told in "tall tales" and ballads quite unknown to the average person living in another part of the country. The speech patterns and idioms are different too — in fact we may say the life styles are different, and this disparity is still present in spite of the homogenizing effects of the mass media.

New knowledge has also tended to develop and perpetuate the variance in cultural values. Such new knowledge is not necessarily that which is discovered in the seats of academia, but may be the acceptance of a new interpretation of a quite well known and accepted truth. For example, new religious sects and cults have sprung up in America to satisfy the disgruntled or those disenchanted with established religions. A quite different example of new knowledge would be the teachings of a health faddist. All of the almost infinite varieties of interpretations and beliefs relating to such basic human concerns as a healthy and satisfying life on this earth as well as a spiritual life after death have collected followers and have added to our cultural pluralism.

A further pluralistic influence is cultural lag (a concept introduced in Chapter Three) and the associated problems of communication between those who accept technological innovation and those who reject it. The development and rise of "bugging" devices for the collection of personal and private information is deemed necessary by some and fundamentally immoral by others. The abandonment of the Latin language in the Mass of the Catholic Church is seen by certain Catholic theologians as a movement to put religious worship back into the hands of the people, but by others as an erosion of the historic church.

It is a well accepted fact among most social theorists that the development and recent rapid growth of urban centers has been a significant factor in increasing cultural pluralism. The "face-to-face" relationships which existed in small-town, rural America have tended to disappear as we have moved into the urban and industrial phase of our society — a fact that is often decried by the romanticists (and the term "romanticists" is not used here in a derogatory sense). An individual living in a small town had to answer to the community for any violation of the socially accepted patterns of behavior, but the city dweller can hide his divergence in the vast sea of divergences that characterizes the urban environment. For the most part, a person can be what he really wants to be in the city without suffering the criticism of the community. In a sense, nobody knows or really cares who or what one is as long as one does not seriously upset the attempts of others to fulfill their own personal aspirations.

To summarize the above points, then, the wide divergence of ethnic and other subcultural groups, the growth of technology and associated cultural lag, the increasing collection of people into urban centers with the related proliferation of alternative styles of life and the growing abandonment of traditional values for a more relativistic morality have produced an America fantastically pluralistic.

SOCIALIZATION AND AMERICAN EDUCATION

The discussion of socialization presented at the beginning of this chapter emphasized the transactional process between the child and his natural and cultural environment. The concepts of heredity, significant symbol, status and role, generalized other, and security system all have importance in terms of the reciproal process by which an individual becomes a personality.

If heredity is the process of the biochemical potentialities of an organism being realized in a particular environment, then, given the uniqueness of human potentiality with an increasing range of environmental circumstances, the possibility of variation in human behavior becomes enormous. There is little question that, within broad limits, the response of human beings to common environmental conditions will be similar, but in terms of specific and particular environmental circumstances we can anticipate only unique responses.

For educators, this concept of the infinite variety of personality possibilities among human beings, despite the seeming commonality of environmental background, is one of the most significant factors in American schools.

Yet education, or more specifically, formal schooling, has been organized on the assumption that children, at given age levels and with generally common backgrounds, respond in common ways, and that any deviation from these anticipated responses is willful, "naughty," or at least against the "best aims" of the school. Often no account has been taken of the growing body of research which indicates that individuals are all different and have different interests, motivations, and goals, to say nothing of different physiological traits. The very structure of the school, with its age-graded system, logically organized curriculum, uniform texts, and standardized tests all speak of modular education instead of "customized" education. Although it may be true that the modular pattern, largely borrowed from industry is more efficient and, in any experiment in mass education such as that which was carried out in the United States in the nineteenth century, perhaps is necessary, the "cult of efficiency" should not dictate a pattern of education which denies most of what we know about human heredity and growth.

CURRENT PROBLEMS IN SOCIALIZATION

As has been indicated earlier, in societies of rapid cultural change, where there are wide variations in ways of behaving, status positions become varied, and the roles which are associated with them become variously interpreted.

Not only is there variation in role interpretation from one individual to another occupying the same status position, but there is also variation in role behavior by the same individual from one period of his life to another. If one were to multiply the increasing number of ways in which roles are played by the growing number of roles one can play in a society, it would not be difficult to see how complex the socialization process can become.

Also, the images available to a child growing up in such a society are many and inconsistent, and the attempt to communicate, in Mead's terms, in such a milieu, is extremely difficult. There is less and less assurance that communication — the ability to call up in another one's own attitudes — is possible when a greater and greater number of interpretations are given to the same significant symbol. And the process of organizing such an array of others, indefinite and changing, into a meaningful generalized other is frustrating and anxiety producing. Who a person is at any given point in time is largely how others define him and how he defines himself in a world of others.

The security system, too, is difficult to maintain in a continually shifting and altering environment, for the ways of satisfying one's needs today may prove to be unsuccessful tomorrow.

"*Imagine a Negro child raised in a community . . . where he is consigned to a rotting section of the community and where he sees his father being discriminated against in employment. . . . The school he attends is a nonreal world fashioned in the image of a white man's dream.*"

Although the situation in America may not be quite as tenuous as the above description implies, nevertheless it would be well to keep it in mind in attempting to understand the behavior of children in contemporary American society.

One further point needs to be made here before we move on. The self-development of the Negro child growing up in a society that is split into two different worlds because of the existence of a caste line based on the color of one's skin is moderated by the degree of social change taking place in his particular environment. If the roles he sees are consistently and clearly played, and interpreted similarly by most of the members of the Negro and white communities, the process of socialization is relatively easy. In some environments, the Negro child learns "his place" and learns to regard himself as inferior to the white, but his world is stable and reliable, and he can adapt to it with considerable security, even if the level at which he lives is just barely sufficient to sustain life.

Now let us shift the situation. Imagine a Negro child raised in a community which is supposedly open, one in which he is continually told that he has the right to fulfill his potentiality, that hard work and sustained effort will allow him to "get ahead," but in which, at the same time, he is consigned to a rotting section of the city where he sees his father being discriminated against in employment and other members of his race being made the butt of crude jokes. The school he attends is a non-real world fashioned in the image of a white man's dream and available only to the white man and a few favored Negroes who have made it. The significant symbols available in his world call up no common responses in the white world. The communication lines are down. Is it any wonder that the two worlds either remain apart in apathy or come together only through hostility and violence? In such an environment of hopelessness, deceit, and cruelty, what can he hope for, who can he believe in, and how does he learn to be kind? The models he uses for self-identification are the crippled selves of his environment.

We must point out here that this contrast of the life styles of Negroes living in different environments is in no sense a defense of the caste system or of the assignment of the Negro to an inferior status but rather a further illustration of the concepts discussed above.

One manifestation of today's youth's withdrawal from society is the Hippie movement. These members are attending a happening in Golden Gate Park, San Francisco, a favorite spot for Hippies in the summer of 1967. The symbols of communication seen here in dress and jewelry have meaning only within this subculture.

This alienation from the mainstream of American society is increasingly seen among other segments of the population as well, as the following chapter attests. The modern world of bureaucracy, technology, and computers is shattering the significant symbols which, in the past, were able to keep the various sectors of the society in communication. In earlier times there may not always have been agreement and consensus between the segments, but at least the meanings were clear. The youth of today, however, more and more appear to be giving up the attempt to communicate. In some, the reaction is hostility, in others, apathy, but whatever the response, one thing is certain: the symbols of communication have various meanings and call up differing responses, and as such a serious chasm is building.

The school has not been effective in keeping communication viable in the past, but it is the only institution in the society which can alter this process of deterioration. If it is to do so, it must itself be altered, and quickly.

SUGGESTIONS FOR FURTHER READING

Friedenberg, Edgar Z. *Coming of Age in America.* New York: Vintage Books, 1967.

Hodgkinson, Harold L. *Education, Interaction, and Social Change.* Englewood Cliffs, N.J.: Prentice-Hall, 1967.

Kardiner, A. *Psychological Frontiers of Society.* New York: Columbia University Press, 1945.

Mayer, Kurt B. *Class and Society.* New York: Random House, 1955.

Mussen, Paul H., John J. Conger, and Jerome Kagan. *Readings in Child Development and Personality.* New York: Harper & Row, 1965.

Ritchie, Oscar W., and Marvin R. Koller. *Sociology of Childhood.* New York: Appleton-Century-Crofts, 1964.

Wallace, Anthony F. C. *Culture and Personality.* New York: Random House, 1961.

The Cry (lithograph by Edvard Munch)

Chapter Five

THE STRUGGLE

AGAINST ALIENATION

As was pointed out in Chapter Four, man resembles all other living organisms in that he is an open biological system in a continuous state of interchange with the physical environment. Through a constant process of inflow and outflow of energy an organism sustains its life. Man, unlike other living organisms, is also an open, "non-organic" system. He must feed upon an interchange of cognitive and affective energies to survive. Without aesthetic, spiritual, intellectual and emotional stimulation from his fellow human beings he cannot become or remain human. Thus, man depends upon groups to achieve his unique form in the hierarchy of life. Indeed, his humanness can be determined solely within a societal context.

Man, the most complex social animal, is also identified by his remarkable and quite perverse propensity for unsocial behavior. Lacking the instinctual characteristics necessary to ensure the preservation of order within his societies and yet dependent upon the survival of societies for his own existence, he creates culture. Culture, the cement that maintains order within societies, is in fact the personality of social systems. It is because of culture that societies can survive the perpetual onslaught of death which eventually immobilizes each of its members.

The knowledge required for survival by a generation of men is not transmitted to his progeny through organic heredity as it is in the case of other animals. Man deliberately and continuously must struggle to ensure that the elements of his cultures which preserve his societies will not perish. Education is his unique way of dealing with the fact that *nature* "tricked" him by providing him with a somewhat ineffective genetic system. *Nurture* furnishes man, a rather physiologically fragile creature, with the "survival kit" needed to preserve the existence of his species.

Social Assimilation and Education

The primary aim of education in all societies is to transmit a "selective brand of civilization" to its members. Each individual within a society must be able not only to identify and describe the personality of his culture but also to internalize it. All aliens, the newly arrived by birth or migration, or those who do not reflect the culture by choice or circumstances must either be rejected or assimilated. Thus, education is primarily the process by which individuals are assimilated through acculturation.

If the process of assimilation is ineffective and the society disintegrates, man must reconstruct a new social order upon different cultural elements. If he fails to perceive the disintegration or inadequately deals with the problem, the personality of the society will suffer from severe psychosis and the society will cease to function. The reader will remember from history that the inability of the individuals within the Holy Roman Empire to develop a communicable culture resulted in a series of internal upheavals which eventually led to the creation of new social orders based upon divergent cultural elements. (In this connection, it may be prudent to recall the old cliché that the Holy Roman Empire was not truly an empire, nor was it Roman, and by no standard could it be labeled holy.)

It has been previously stated that man creates cultures in order to survive. It is important to emphasize that the creator of culture is man and that the life of a society is rooted in its members. The previous remark that a society possesses a personality does not mean to imply an organismic conception of society. The society does not exist as an entity separate from its members. It is its members. If the personality of the culture suffocates the personalities of the individuals within its boundaries, it will cut itself off from the very source of its life and will die. The history of the Spartan society after the "Great Refusal," when Spartan leaders began developing a "barracks state," is illustrative of this phenomenon of societal suicide. Cutting itself off from the dynamism of continuous regeneration by stifling creativity and innovation, the Spartans were unable to preserve the "life" of their culture. Atrophy set in and the death knell announced the demise of an already rigid corpse.

Two important conclusions relevant to an analysis of the educational endeavor can be drawn from the previous discussion. First, assimilation through acculturation is a central aim of education within all societies. If the formal or informal educational endeavor fails to bring about assimilation, the society will disintegrate. Second, if the society is over-assimilated and if education fails to preserve individual creative powers, it will also perish. The key to man's survival, therefore, is to discover the "happy mean" between sociological assimilation and the preservation of the individual's autonomy. The reason for the plethora of disagreements and discussions concerning major social, political, economic, and educational issues during the twentieth century, and indeed throughout man's brief history on this planet, is due to the fact that the "happy mean" between sociological assimilation and the preservation of individual autonomy cannot be readily identified. That which is identified by one man as "disintegration of society," another labels "individual freedom," and conversely, what is viewed by some as "assimilation," others identify as "destructive collectivism or groupism." When such conflicting views become the ideologies of warring factions, reason oftentimes cannot salve the resultant wounds.

THE BIRTH OF THE SCHOOL

As discussed in Chapter Three, in primitive societies the process of education is simple and informal. Aboriginal parents, assisted by the frequently disenchanted tribal priest, carry the burden of ensuring that their children will acquire the correct behavior traits. What the young fail to learn about their culture from the parents and the priests they learn by observing and participating in tribal activities. In ancient times, the knowledge the tribe accumulated formed the aboriginal curriculum. As the pool of knowledge deepened and broadened, men, in their persistent search for order, developed a categorical system and the disciplines were born. As the categories of knowledge increased and as men acquired diverse and sophisticated ways of knowing, the task of educating was shared by an increasing number of specialists.

It is worthy of note that the development of knowledge is exponential in nature. Not only does the discovery of new knowledge increase the possibility of creating more knowledge (e.g., the discovery of systems of optics and the resultant discovery of the worlds hidden from man's limited perception), but it also is accompanied by an increase in the division of labor within social systems. The reader will remember from the discussion of roles in Chapter Four that as individuals assume more specialized roles, a growing complexity of behavioral expectations related to these roles are included within the body of knowledge to be transmitted to the individuals within the society. To illustrate the latter assertion, in the tribal society individuals who assumed roles related to political functions, such as members of tribal councils, were required to learn behavior patterns associated with their specialty. Not only did they generally have to wear distinct clothing, as do our court justices, but they also had to deal with individuals within the tribe according to specified rules and regulations. The well known "rites of passage" usually were followed by specified behavioral expectations. Some societies, such as the pre-communist Chinese society, developed extensive and detailed ceremonial patterns. Although modern societies lack these ceremonial expectations, they are characterized by an increase in specialization and a plethora of specific behavioral expectations due to roles and status. Individuals are expected to behave according to their roles and resultant normative expectancies. A successful librarian, for example, generally behaves according to different norms than does an airline stewardess. Although general behavioral expectations are not necessarily verbalized to the degree that are the norms of specified roles, every society has an unsung Amy Vanderbilt.

As social systems and systems of knowledge grew more complex, the informal educational process became inadequate and was institutionalized through the creation of the school. Although the informal educational system continues to operate, the advent of the industrial revolution, the creation of nation-states, the migration of large groups of individuals from one society to another, the replacement of the extended family by the nuclear family, and the explosion of knowledge has caused the school to assume a more vital and central role in the process of acculturation. Yet to be resolved is the delineation of the educational responsibilities of the family, social and religious agencies, the school, and the recent arrival upon the educational scene, mass media. Whether the family's role in the educational endeavor will continue to decline as the culture becomes more homogenized will depend upon the nature of the evolving social structure and culture. What is evident, however, is that the school, the offspring of society, is assigned the major role in the task of acculturation. The school exists to teach the culture to the young so that they will "fit" within the society. It will be judged successful if the individuals attending it behave in a manner that reveals that they have internalized the essential elements of the culture. If they behave differently from the expectations determined by the cultural norms (the conscience of the society), they will be viewed as "criminal intruders" and the school's ability to perform its assigned task will be questioned. The teachers will have to successfully explain the *raison d'etre* for the school's apparent failure, reeducate their masters, migrate, or drink hemlock.

A question often cited and worthy of note is whether the school has a responsibility to change the social order. It is a moot question in a homogeneous society, for such a society preserves the life-sustaining umbilical cord between itself and the school by placing the school under the control of successfully acculturated individuals and by selecting teachers who reflect the cultural norms. The question is relevant, however, in a pluralistic society with a heterogeneous culture. In such a society, exemplified by the United States, the school may become the center to which divergent societal impulses may be focused. The Progressive Movement in American education, for example, reflected the progressive impulse that existed within certain segments of the society. Whether the school "ought" to assist in changing the social order is another matter, and the reader must arrive at his own conclusion.

THE SCHOOL AS A MIRROR OF THE PERSONALITY
OF THE SOCIETY

As previously mentioned, assimilation through acculturation is
an integral aspect of education in all societies. Each society, however, has a plethora of cultural ideals which are unique to it, as
Kluckhohn has succinctly stated:

> Some of each child's wants are those common to all human
> animals. But each culture has its own scheme for the most de-
> sirable and the most approved ways of satisfying these needs.[1]

Each culture reflects central ideals which become the guiding
principles for all societal activities. The previously mentioned
Spartans, for example, prized physical rigor and obedience to the
state, while the early American colonists in the New England
Bible states valued spiritual rigor and obedience to the "Word of
God."

Before taking a look at some twentieth century American ideals,
the reader should be alerted to the fact that the "happy mean"
between assimilation and the preservation of individual autonomy
is usually located within a zone on a continuum that is determined
by the culture. A totalitarian state emphasizes the assimilation
factor, while a democratic state stresses the preservation of the
autonomy of the individual. Also, not all societies have the same
degree of integration. Modern industrial societies generally are
more extended in size, include a greater diversity of peoples, and
are based upon a variety of cultures. To deal with the phenomenon of "loose integration," assimilation assumes diverse forms and
characteristics. The concept of nationalism, for example, was a
significant factor during the emergence of modern mass societies,
and its emotional expression of patriotism continues as a vital element in the process of assimilation.

THE AMERICAN IDEAL OF INDIVIDUALISM

Any attempt to identify specific cultural elements within a
society as complex and pluralistic as the United States is filled
with pitfalls. The following is solely an attempt to identify some
general principles which follow from the ideal of individualism.

[1] Clyde Kluckhohn, *Mirror for Man* (New York: Fawcett World Library, 1965), p. 171.

Rather than attempting to provide a brief definition of this concept, a task comparable to the search for the philosopher's stone, the following essential elements are provided to assist the reader in an understanding of the nature of individualism:

1. Groups are the sum total of individuals, and individuals are the primary agent, not the group *per se.*

2. Individuals are expected to deviate from adjusted patterns, although such deviations may be partially controlled by existing patterns.

3. The feelings, potential, and limitations of the individual are recognized and respected.

4. The individual is a source of creativity — the ability to discover meaningful ways to relate reality.

5. An individual's right to privacy and solitude is not abridged or denied.

6. Loyalty to a group must be derived from a desire to be part of a group and not from a desire for unity for its own sake.

7. Inner values and ideals that conflict with those of the majority of individuals within a group must be respected without threat of coercion for the purpose of assuring group cohesion.

8. The freedom to select friends and values cannot be abridged by forced "gladhandism."

9. A mature individual must be prepared to assume the responsibility of choosing his own goals.

10. An individual finds his own meaning within a group without being dependent upon it for security.

The "democratic creed" is rooted in the concept of individualism. Society enhances man's ability to become human. A basic American tenet which flows from the ideal of individualism is that the individual should be provided with the maximum opportunity to realize his potential. The social, political, and economic systems within the American society are defended on this basis.

In a political sense, individualism means that the individual is superior to the state and that the individuals who govern the state obtain their right to govern from the governed. The right of the majority is avowed, but, in order to protect the minority from the possible perfidy of the majority, the minority's rights are protected by law.

In the social sphere, individualism rests upon the concept of class mobility within a class society. The Marxist ideal of a classless society is rejected because it is thought to inhibit the individual's chances to achieve and be rewarded according to his ability and determination. Thus, the opportunity for migration from one class to another provides the rationale for the defense of the class structure. The often cited examples of "poverty to riches" reflect the conviction that a class society differs markedly from a caste system. The dominant middle class in American society sets the general patterns of behavioral expectations and, indeed, is the source of the essential elements that make up the culture. To be American in the fullest sense is to reflect middle class values.

The American democratic creed is expressed in the economic system labeled "capitalism." The right of the individual to earn according to his "ability" and to "gather to himself the goods of the earth" is viewed as the basis of an economic democracy. The right of private property belongs to both consumer and capitalist. As the industrial revolution progresses, the stock market is gradually replacing the small town market place as the symbol of a democratic economic system in action.

The above description of individualism as an American ideal is not intended to imply that the ideal is necessarily reflected in practice. Discrepancies often occur, and if they persist, they cause social crises. An illustration of such a pattern of unrest is the great labor upheaval during the decade following World War I. The widespread labor strikes resulted in part from the failure and apparent inherent inability of the existing capitalistic system to provide equality of economic opportunity. While the rich were increasing their wealth, the poor remained in poverty, and the workers demanded that the ideals upheld by the society be put into practice. Eventually, alterations were made in the existing capitalistic system, accompanied by an extension of federal government activity in the economic domain.

The Negro sit-ins and marches of the sixties provide another vivid example of the crisis that results when a social system fails to implement the ideals that are integral to its culture. Because a significant segment of the populace, led by the august Supreme Court (the institutionalized conscience of the society), realized that our avowed devotion to political equality and equality of opportunity was ludicrous in comparison with current social practices, the implementation of much-needed reforms was demanded.

The dilemma concerning whether "American democratic ideals" can indeed be implemented in a modern mass society has been the source of diverse tracts and tomes. A study of the concepts of economic freedom, social class, and political equality, when placed in juxtaposition, presents various perplexing questions. Can economic freedom, with its obvious correlate that some will be richer than others, exist simultaneously with political equality whereby each man has an equal voice in the process of operating his government? Indeed, more basic questions are: Can the ideals implied by sociological assimilation and the preservation of individualism be realized simultaneously? and Can equality exist in any sphere of human activity when nature appears to have been rather remiss in distributing assets and liabilities? The advocates of the "democratic creed" generally answer these frustrating questions in the affirmative. The ideals are not only viewed as theoretically compatible but also capable of being effectively implemented. This American faith is derived, in part, from a belief in our capacity to affect our future and the concurrent rejection of the concept of an overpowering *destino*. Our faith in nurture overshadows our fear of the limitations imposed upon us by nature. Indeed, we can reflect upon man's past journey and argue that he is ornery enough to succeed. From the day when he arose from the primeval muck to the present hour, he has confounded the gods.

This American faith in man's eventual success is also based upon our conviction that education is the panacea that will overcome his organic limitations. It is reflected in Thomas Jefferson's letter to George Wythe in 1786. He asserted: "I think by far the most important bill in our whole code is that for the diffusion of knowledge among the people. No other sure foundation can be devised for the preservation of freedom and happiness."[2]

THE TASKS OF THE SCHOOL

The school in American society is assigned two central tasks: (1) the assimilation by acculturation of the neophytes within the society, and (2) the preservation of the autonomy of the indi-

[2] Gordon C. Lee (ed.), *Crusade Against Ignorance* (Richmond, Va.: The William Byrd Press, 1962), p. 99.

vidual in a mode reflective of the ideal of individualism discussed above. The assertion that assimilation by acculturation is a central task of the school does not mean that the school rejects the goal of education for world society mentioned in Chapter One. The nation-state is linked with the world community. Nationalism and internationalism are not mutually exclusive. Acculturation will include elements which relate to the world community. As assimilation in the American nation-state implies an acceptance of the social unit labeled *family*, it also may include the goal of integrating the young into the world community.

The remainder of this chapter will deal with the difficulty of accomplishing these ends in twentieth century American society; it will also identify some difficulties encountered by the schools in their attempts to fulfill their two central tasks. The failure to bring about effective sociological assimilation will be viewed in reference to ethnic and social class differences. The failure to implement some of the ideals of individualism will be analyzed by focusing upon the social forces that threaten the autonomy of individuals by fragmenting their identity. Individuals who are thus sociologically non-assimilated and/or psychologically fragmented may be said to be suffering from alienation.

Alienation in American Society

The meaning of the word "alienation" is elusive; a cursory examination of its use shows that a variety of definitions abound. For the purpose of this chapter, however, it will be defined as a separation or a sense of separation from one's "real self" or from other human beings with whom the individual interacts. An individual is alienated if he cannot fathom his own "within" or his identity as a person. He is also alienated if he is unable to effectively communicate with other human beings within his environment. Both forms of alienation prevent the individual from being or feeling "human"; they keep him from becoming an integrated whole capable of interchanging cognitive and affective energies with other persons in his environment. The two forms of alienation that will be focused upon are (1) alienation resulting from the failure of assimilation, which will be labeled *sociological alienation,* and (2) alienation that results from the loss of an individual's autonomy, that is, the fragmentation of the self, which will be called *psychological alienation*.

These two forms of alienation have diverse causes, but two basic causes can be identified. First, alienation that results from *nature* (e.g., congenital mental retardation), and secondly, that which results from *nurture* (e.g., cultural deviation).

SOCIOLOGICAL ALIENATION

In order to be assimilated within the American society, a foreign-born individual must not only effectively adjust to the general American cultural patterns and ideals but he must also be integrated within the dominant social class, the middle class. Thus, to be assimilated within the American society, an individual must successfully perform inter-societal migration by adopting the cultural norms of his new native country, and he must also successfully migrate from the lower socio-economic class to the dominant middle class. The success of intra-societal migration towards the middle class is due in great measure to the degree in which an individual internalizes the general cultural norms (e.g., the democratic creed). Unless he completes both forms of migration, he remains an alien. The schema shown in Figure 2 represents the phenomenon of assimilation.

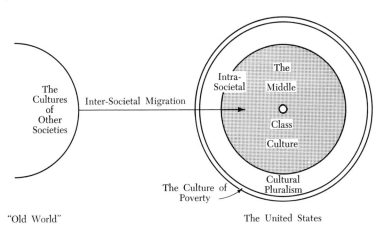

FIGURE 2

The Process of Cultural Assimilation

Successful assimilation implies that an individual migrating from an "Old World" society eventually becomes an acceptable member of the middle class. In other words, in order to become "an American," an immigrant must often migrate through the lowest, poorest social class, through a society composed of separate but not equal ethnic groups, and eventually assume a somewhat stable position within the middle class. Thus, many individuals must divest themselves of a variety of normative elements and expectations derived from the "Old World" culture, accept and eventually reject the culture of poverty, sustain a transformed ethnic culture, and ultimately internalize middle class values and behavioral expectations. Not all aliens need pass through all of the areas identified in Figure 2, however. The speed and nature of assimilation within the middle class society rest in part upon the similarity and dissimilarity between the original and the adopted culture. An Englishman, for example, may migrate directly from the "Old World" culture into middle class American society. Also, an individual may be native to the American society and yet remain within the outer core of the middle class societal milieu. Although assimilation can be obtained by extending the middle class culture to include subcultural elements by diversifying acceptable normative elements and modifying behavioral expectations, the process generally rests upon a conscious attempt to acculturate the aliens to existing patterns.

The Immigrants. As far back as the founding of the American Republic the problem imposed by inter-societal migration has been of central concern to the schools. The United States, being a nation composed of immigrants and the progeny of immigrants, faced a somewhat unique struggle to achieve assimilation. Unable to develop a sense of attachment to the elusive concept, "fatherland," the cohesive force which was to unite the American people was the religion of democracy. As the immigrants arrived on the American shores from diverse lands and cultures, they were gathered into the educational ladle, the public school system, and dipped into the great Melting Pot. Thus, a form of nationalism, rooted in the democratic creed and taught in the English language, was the unifying agent. The American form of assimilation was based upon the assumption that as ethnic differences disappeared

the "American type" would be generated. The school was assigned the task of amalgamating and Americanizing the peoples
of the "New Jerusalem." It is important to note that the so-called
"American type" (a term reflective of the middle class culture)
was not truly an amalgam but rather a microcosmic mirror that
reflected the "evolved" culture introduced by the earliest immigrants. Could it be that the Melting Pot was to produce a fuzzy
replica of an Englishman?

The offspring of many of the immigrants, especially those of
second and third generations, with assistance from the public
school, successfully overthrew the subcultures of the ethnic ghettoes and entered the middle class society. Though the public
school watched with deep satisfaction the Americanization of the
neophytes, there was often a conscious and unconscious opposition

Inter-societal migrants. An Italian family at Ellis Island, 1905.

to such a process on the part of the immigrants. The ethnic ghettoes the immigrants frequently established reflected their understandable fear of becoming isolated aliens within the yet-to-be-internalized adopted culture. The family social unit often became the focal point of the pressure to resist acculturation.

In recent years a new concept appeared which challenges the Melting Pot idea of assimilation. The advocates of this concept, "cultural pluralism," want to preserve ethnic differences. Cultural pluralism implies that the diverse cultures which are represented by the variety of ethnic groups who settled on the American soil should be preserved and protected from the process of cultural diffusion. Thus, as oil and water placed within one container do not mix, the diverse cultures would be contained by one nation but would not be adulterated by each other.

Although cultural pluralism continues to exist for a limited period after the arrival and settlement of immigrants, it rarely endures beyond the third generation. When it does exist, it usually does not permeate the middle class society. The values and behavioral expectations reflected by the members of the middle class are remarkably similar. Although minor ideological differences often result in controversy, these differences result primarily because the middle class culture is a hybrid culture.

Although cultural pluralism appears to be more suited to a pluralistic and democratic society, its workability in twentieth century America is questionable. Would members of the diverse ethnic groups have equal access to the rungs of the socioeconomic ladder, or would those individuals whose cultures more closely resemble that of the individuals who have already reached the top have a better chance of economic success? Would such an approach to the assimilation process result in centers of highly homogeneous subcultures, preventing the development of a suitable all-encompassing culture that would be adequate to sustain order within society? Also, the problem of cultural suitability is of central concern. A culture that has evolved within environmental conditions radically different from those found in America and within a different historical context cannot be "transplanted" without significant alterations. The colonists who arrived in the seventeenth century, for example, although dedicated to the preservation of the culture of their fathers, were forced to transform integral elements to adjust to the frontier environment of their adopted homeland. Although the culture of the nascent American society was quite similar to its English antecedent, it was also significantly different from it, because of the pressure of environmental factors. Illustrative of this assertion is the breakdown of the apprenticeship system in the early colonies.

In spite of the diverse approaches to an understanding of assimilation, however, the fact is that assimilation must occur if the society is to be preserved. It is only the form the assimilation should take which remains in dispute.

The American Indians. The original inhabitants of the land, the American Indians, are in the rather paradoxical position of being aliens in their own land. During the early years of colonization by the Europeans, sporadic yet zealous missionary attempts to assimilate the Indians were made. The names of early agencies dedicated to the task of assimilation, such as the Anglican Society for the Propagation of the Gospel in Foreign Parts, betray the commitment to Christianize the red man. Because of the Indians' courageous stamina in resisting the pressures to destroy their cultures, and because of the federal government's policy of segregating the Indians under the guise of federal protection, however, they continue to be sociologically alienated from the "American" culture. Under the government's policy of *de facto* apartheid, our aborigines remain outside the middle class culture and often outside the economic structure. Whether the Indian eventually will obtain the recognition he deserves for his unique status and ways remains to be seen. The pseudo-recognition he receives by visitors on holiday when he is encouraged to display the exotic aspects of his culture is an American tragedy.

The American Negro. The American Negro, involuntarily brought to these shores shortly after the arrival of the first settlers, remained in slavery throughout the early centuries of our history. Treated as property and deprived of control over his own destiny until the mid-1860's, he was unable to preserve his African cultures or to develop an American Negro culture, since slavery inhibits the development of culture. Once freed, he was prevented from being assimilated into the middle class society and forced to become a part of the social class which reflected the culture of economic deprivation.

The assertion that there does not exist an American Negro culture is not meant to imply that Negro citizens have not contributed significantly to the American culture. It merely means that the shading of one's skin cannot be the cause of the creation of a culture. Admittedly, the behavioral expectations that result from the perception of "color" as a significant factor may result in *some* shared ways of behaving. However, such shared ways, unless combined with various other factors, do not bring about the creation of a culture. The poor Negro who inhabits an agrarian southern community more closely resembles his white brother living in similar circumstances than other Negroes living in a more affluent environment. (The reason that the American Negro is "different" is not because of nature but rather because of nurture. He is different solely because nurture has caused some individuals to *perceive* color as a relevant determiner of human patterns of interaction. Thus, an insignificant but visible characteristic has forced *some* Negroes to remain within the lowest socioeconomic class.)

Recent developments seem to indicate that certain Negroes, deprived of middle class status and forced to live within a class identified by economic deprivation, are seeking to establish a subculture which, indeed, would serve as a protector in a hostile world. Thus a minority of Negroes have adopted the Muslim faith, along with selected elements from African cultures. That this new lifestyle will free them from the culture of poverty is questionable.

The Poor. The most readily identified as alienated because of social class are the poor. (One could argue that the very rich [see Figure 2], are equally alienated from the middle class as the members of the American international jet set have demonstrated. But the society in general and the members of that subgroup are not about to make their alienation an educational issue.)

Often deprived of political equality and frequently prevented by circumstance from moving out of the lowest socioeconomic class, the poor have failed to implement the concept of assimilation. John Steinbeck's vivid descriptions of the poverty of the inhabitants of the Dust Bowl during the thirties and the recent exposés of the plight of the peoples of Appalachia and of the migrant

A poor white family of Appalachia.

Farmer and son await relief check.

Negro child in slum.

workers of California, Florida, and other fruit- and vegetable-
growing areas offer moving accounts of the appalling suffering imposed by poverty.

The culture of poverty is fashioned with its own set of values
and behavioral expectations. As the values of all cultures represent methods of survival in a hostile environment, the values of
the poor are designed to enable them to survive in a sociologically
hostile world.

Because of the nature of technological change which increasingly creates a demand for skilled workers, and the need to make
effective use of the formal educational process, the poor have been
stratified within a class that closely resembles a caste. The school
has become the agency which may best serve to liberate the individuals involuntarily enslaved by economic deprivation, but, unfortunately, it includes elements which inhibit its attempt to successfully accomplish the task of assimilating these individuals.
As an agency of the middle class society, the school sets middle
class goals and expectations for the students, and achievement
and external reward depend upon the degree to which these values
are learned and internalized. The problem goes beyond that of
learning to read, write, and compute, as Talcott Parsons has ob-
served:

> The criteria of the achievement are generally speaking, un-
> differentiated into the cognitive and technical component and
> the moral or 'social' component. But with respect to its bearing
> on societal values, it is broadly a differentiation of levels of ca-
> pacity to act in accord with these values.[3]

The road to advancement within the societal milieu increasingly depends upon the school's capacity to provide the maximum
educational opportunity for all its students. As pointed out in
Chapter 2, the goal of equalizing educational opportunity cannot
be easily achieved. The problem is being tackled by an increasingly active federal government and by many educators committed
to unearthing the roots of the dilemma. The recent increase in
federal monies for education is due, in part, to the desire to assist
the poor in becoming assimilated into the middle class. Whether

[3] Talcott Parsons, "The School as a Social System," *Harvard Educational Review* (Fall, 1959), p. 300.

a similar attempt will be made to develop a more heterogeneous culture which will include the values of groups peripheral to the middle class remains to be seen. According to Horatio Ulibarri,

> The schools have been complacent to a large degree in presenting only a small aspect of the American culture, namely, the middle-class values and orientations, as the sum total of the curricula in the schools.[4]

The effectiveness of the school in assimilating the children and youth of lower socioeconomic classes will depend upon the empathy of the teachers and the opportunity for cross-cultural contact. Teachers must also be prepared to accept prescribed innovations which are not solely based upon sound analyses of existing situations and needed reform, but also based upon a courageous attempt to remove the middle class "tunnel vision" of reality.

Other Sociologically Alienated Groups. The school, of course, must also continue its task of assimilating all of the neophytes for, indeed, all children are born alien to society. Even the task of assimilating children of middle class parents into the middle class society is difficult and frustrating. As the culture evolves with increasing rapidity and as the institutions within the society are altered to "fit" technological advances, the task of assimilation requires greater wisdom and finesse. Assimilation in twentieth century America implies that an individual must not only fit into the existing society but must also be capable of fitting himself into a society which, as yet, does not exist and cannot be accurately described.

Before turning to the problem of psychological alienation which follows, the reader should be aware that there are various other types of sociological alienation that are relevant to the educational endeavor. Those individuals, for example, stigmatized by a physical or emotional handicap, often unsuccessfully struggle to be assimilated within the society, while artists and intellectuals must perpetually struggle to feel a sense of belonging in a society characterized by a reward system based upon static norms and rigid

[4] Horatio Ulibarri, "Teacher Awareness of Sociocultural Differences in the Multicultural Classrooms," *Sociology and Social Research* (October, 1960), p. 49.

determinants of achievement. Although the special problems of
handicapped and gifted children have received increasing recognition among educators in recent years, they are still given too
little attention in many school systems.

Psychological Alienation

We must point out at the outset of this discussion of psychological alienation that sociological alienation and psychological
alienation cannot, in fact, be readily separated; often they are concomitant.

Psychological alienation exists when an individual fails to preserve or to develop his autonomy. He becomes solely a conditioned
reactor rather than a free actor within the societal milieu; he
cannot internalize the elements of individualism listed in an
earlier section of this chapter. Psychological alienation results,
in part, from the inability of an individual to cope with the mass,
corporate society. Indeed, the fragmentation of identity often results from the demands imposed upon an individual by a society
revolutionized by technological advances. As Fromm says, "Man
has created a world of man-made things as it never existed before.
He has constructed a complicated social machine to administer
the technical machine he built."[5]

In the following pages we will describe briefly some of the
aspects of twentieth century American society which have encouraged the development of psychological alienation.

The Isolation of the Worker. The nature of our industrialized
society has greatly limited the individual's opportunity to share
cognitive and affective energies with other human beings (a vital
factor in developing and sustaining an awareness of one's identity). The centralization of the giants of the industrial world has
generated the megalopolis and isolated industrial parks. Thus, the
worker, a veritable gypsy, is forced to migrate perpetually between
the suburban community where he lives and the great cities of
Babel surrounding the industrial towers of the twentieth century
where he works. As a result of this phenomenon, he frequently

[5] Erich Fromm, "Alienation under Capitalism," in *Man Alone: Alienation in Modern Society,* eds. Eric Josephson and Mary Josephson (New
York: Dell Publishing Co., 1962), p. 59.

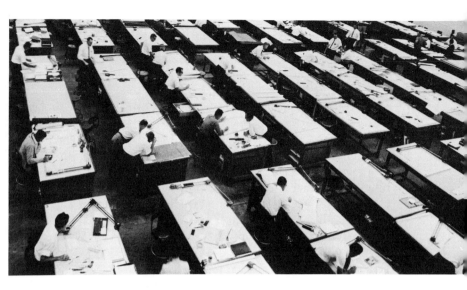

Drafting engineers. Even highly trained men can seem insignificant in a large company like this one.

cannot develop meaningful interactions with other human beings. Indeed, he cannot communicate. Max Lerner, in describing the character of the American city dweller, writes:

> It has been psychologically hardened by innumerable brief encounters — in public schools, on subways and buses, in restaurants, in the course of shopping — which would become intolerable if one did not sheathe oneself against them with a constricted response.[6]

Thus, the modern urbanite-suburbanite often cannot discover meaning within his fluid community. He encounters his family for brief interludes; his home often resembles a boarding house; and his neighborhood, with its well-paved streets and well-mowed lawns, seems to lack the movement and feeling of "real life."

As he moves to the suburbs to regain contact with nature, he shortens his days by increasing the "lost hours" enroute between home and office or factory. Eventually, the tentacles of the ravenous megalopolis will reach out and encompass his new haven. Indeed, in his sense of alienation, the modern American resembles Adam and Eve in the Garden of Eden. He, however, differs from

[6] Max Lerner, *America as a Civilization* (New York: Simon and Schuster, 1961), p. 168.

his ancestors who consumed the "forbidden fruit" because he suffers from the realization that he has chopped down the "tree of life" and replaced it with a parking lot.

A highly industrialized society is also characterized by an increase in the division of labor. Both the white-collar and the blue-collar worker are required to perform a highly specialized and often monotonous task, and instead of working cooperatively with others in a joint endeavor, each works alone, separated from the opportunity for meaningful interaction with fellow workers. He is also deprived of the satisfaction of releasing his creative urge; unlike the skilled worker-artist of bygone days, the modern worker seldom experiences the joy of seeing the results of his special, individual labor in the finished product. He realizes, too, that the product will soon be obsolete and, even more discouraging, that his job may become obsolete — that automation may soon invade his domain and replace him.

The Fragmentation of the Self. As the role relationships within the corporate structure become more complex and static, the worker must assume a pattern of behavior which is determined by the needs of an efficiency-oriented sub-social system. Indeed, the autonomous, inner-directed individual so vividly described by David Riesman is often viewed as a liability in the corporate world. The mass society appears to rest upon the shoulders of the other-directed man, who is willing to perform in accordance with the variety of behavioral expectations of the corporate society. Eventually, however, this individual begins to see himself only through the roles he plays, and his identity becomes fragmented. He may be an industrial worker, a union steward, a member of the bowling league, but never an integrated whole — a man.

Besides having his name replaced by his social security number as the badge of his identity, the worker's integrity and his right to privacy are curtailed by a barrage of "psychological" tests which he is required to complete in order to assure that he will find his "proper place" in the complex maze of a bureaucratic, industrial complex.

The Search for Stability. Since man is a moral agent who can transcend himself, he perpetually seeks guidelines for his judgments and actions. In order to "be," he must be free to make choices, but to make choices, he must have alternatives from which to choose. In twentieth century America, however, as the culture has become more homogenized, and as diverse normative elements have become integral to the culture, values have become increasingly nebulous. Without identifiable values or norms, the quest for identity becomes more chaotic and frustrating.

The prevailing social philosophy of relativism also tends to increase psychological alienation. The ancient Aristotelian search for truth, the scholastic search for truth, and the Newtonian search for natural laws have been replaced by a relativistic concept of reality, which has as its focus the process of critical thinking. Although this development has led to a more rational understanding of reality, it often results in destructive skepticism.

Another factor which, in some ways, has led to a diminishing sense of self is the growth of science. As we probe into the universe, our search for identity is confounded by the realization that we are microscopic creatures within our own galaxy. We can but muse over the possible psychological effects of our sojourn into space and the resultant realization that we are but specks upon a speck within a gargantuan complex ocean.

THE SCHOOL AND ALIENATION

The school must ensure that the ideal of individualism be sustained while adequately preparing individuals to fit into the modern mass corporate society. The manner in which it will meet its task will determine, in part, the nature of the future social order. The way in which the school has tackled its tasks in the past has been generally reactive rather than initiative; it has usually awaited cues from the society. The rest of this section provides a possible pattern by which the school could (not necessarily "should") deal with the two basic forms of alienation.

The present educational endeavor contains the threads of this pattern: (1) the integration of individuals within the schools who are alienated because of *nurture* so that they will be assimilated into the adult society, and (2) the segregation of individuals within the schools who are alienated because of *nature* for the same purpose — social assimilation. Thus, when society is responsible for the alienation, the aliens may be integrated within the school. The development of the comprehensive school, for example, results in the integration of individuals from diverse ethnic groups and social classes. Also, the recent Supreme Court rulings in which the "separate but equal" approach to race relations has been reversed implies the concept "integration in school for assimilation in society."

Individuals who are alienated because of nature, on the other hand, may be separated from their non-alienated peers in order to become a part of special programs for their benefit. The development of the field of exceptional education is an example of this practice. Thus, by specializing the instruction of the exceptional child, he is being assisted in dealing with a "maladjustment" imposed upon him by nature.

The above pattern for dealing with alienated children and youth, needless to say, is not clearly defined, nor is it universally accepted by educators. It has been introduced here solely as a point of departure for further analysis and discussion. The problems presented by such a scheme are many. First, the differences between nature and nurture cannot be clearly distinguished. Second, the ideals of the society must be reflected in practice. For example, should the gifted child be sectioned within the school? If one answers in the affirmative, he may be labeled anti-democratic for advocating an elitist concept of education. On the other hand, if his reply is negative, he can also be labeled undemocratic, for the integration of a gifted child with "normal" children could imply that the former would not be granted an opportunity to make maximum use of his special abilities.

Conclusion

A final word should be added concerning the nature of the dilemma of alienation. Although the previous assertions may seem to indicate that modern man is a failure, the opposite is, perhaps, closer to the truth. The very fact that he can ask himself questions dealing with his own identity and his place within the universe is evidence of success in other areas of life. The reader may recall that man's journey through history has involved a persistent struggle to meet his most basic needs in a very hostile physical environment. Today, in twentieth century America, because most of us have succeeded so well in providing for our primary physical wants, we are now free to search for greater fulfillment. The malaise of this age may therefore be attributed not only to our complex social order, but also to the increase of leisure time during which we can ask ourselves the questions a great majority of our ancestors were not able to formulate.

In other words, though we cannot deny that modern man is maladjusted, we must agree with M.V.C. Jeffreys that

> It is because man is maladjusted that he is unique in Nature. From his maladjustment — evident in the chasm between aspiration and capacity, vision and performance — spring all the distinctively human activities; scientific inquiry, artistic creation, philosophical speculation, and — the supporting condition of them all — historical experience.[7]

SUGGESTIONS FOR FURTHER READING

Coleman, James S. *The Adolescent Society.* New York: The Free Press of Glencoe, 1961.

Fischer, Louis, and Donald R. Thomas. *Social Foundations of Educational Decisions.* Belmont, Calif.: Wadsworth Publishing Company, 1965.

Goffman, Erving. *Stigma: Notes on the Management of Spoiled Identity.* Englewood Cliffs, N. J.: Prentice-Hall, 1963.

Josephson, Eric, and Mary Josephson. *Man Alone: Alienation in Modern Society.* New York: Dell Publishing Co., 1962.

Keniston, Kenneth. *The Uncommitted: Alienated Youth in American Society.* New York: Harcourt, Brace & World, 1965.

Kerber, August, and Barbara Bommarito (eds.). *The Schools and the Urban Crisis.* New York: Holt, Rinehart & Winston, 1965.

Lucio, William H. (ed.). *Readings in American Education.* Chicago: Scott, Foresman & Company, 1963.

Riesman, David. *Individualism Reconsidered.* Garden City, N.Y.: Doubleday & Company, 1954.

Shapiro, Harry L. (ed.). *Man, Culture and Society.* New York: Oxford University Press, 1964.

[7] M. V. C. Jeffreys, *Personal Values in the Modern World* (Baltimore: Penguin Books, 1962), p. 9.

A Peace Corps volunteer in Liberia.

Chapter Six

EDUCATION AND THE
EMERGING WORLD
COMMUNITY

Lewis Mumford, in *The Human Prospect,* writes,

> Each of us must remember his humanness; it takes precedence over our race, our economic class, our politics, our religion, or our nationality. Only to the extent that the nations cultivate this humanness, becoming members one of another, can our civilization achieve peace and security, to say nothing of the well-being and creativeness that will eventually issue forth from them.[1]

To preserve his humanness, and indeed to survive, man lives in groups. Each individual belonging to the species labeled *homo sapiens* is nurtured as an integral part of social units. Man not only develops a sense of his self as being separate from that of other selves, but he also sees himself as a part of a greater self. As Hans Kohn has said, "The mental life of man is as much dominated by an ego-consciousness as it is by a group-consciousness."[2] The socialization process is an essential aspect of man's

---

[1] Lewis Mumford, *The Human Prospect* (Carbondale, Ill.: Southern Illinois University Press, 1965), p. 257.

[2] Hans Kohn, *The Idea of Nationalism* (New York: The Macmillan Co., 1961), p. 11.

physical, emotional, and cognitive development. Indeed, "individual and associative aspects of the unitary human being"[3] cannot be separated.

Communities and Societies

The size, structure, functions, norms, and behavioral expectations of the diverse groups to which an individual may belong vary according to the reason or reasons for the relationships among the individuals who compose the group. The two most basic types of social units to which human beings belong are *communities* and *societies*. The differences between the two are central to an understanding of the problems encountered in an attempt to educate for world perspective.

According to the philosopher Jacques Maritain, a community is "a product of instinct and heredity in given circumstances and historical frameworks. . . ."[4] To Maritain, a community *exists* prior to an act of cognition or will and *results* from a fact (e.g., geographical proximity) which creates "a common unconscious psyche, common feelings, and psychological structures, and common mores."[5]

Alex Inkeles, a sociologist, defines the word "community" in a strikingly similar fashion:

> The *essence* of community is a sense of common bond, the sharing of an identity, membership in a group holding some things, physical or spiritual, in common esteem, coupled with the acknowledgement of rights and obligations with reference to all others so identified.[6]

The degree to which a "sense of common bond" is expressed will vary according to the type of community and the circumstances which affect the intensity of the interaction among its members.

[3] John Dewey, "The Crisis in Human History: Danger of Retreat to Individualism," *Commentary* (March, 1946), p. 2.

[4] Jacques Maritain, *Man and the State* (Chicago: The University of Chicago Press, 1957), p. 4.

[5] *Ibid.*, p. 3.

[6] Alex Inkeles, *What Is Sociology?* (Englewood Cliffs, N.J.: Prentice-Hall, 1965), p. 69.

In fact, as Inkeles says, some communities may be latent, that is, "having merely a potential for common action."[7]

The world community of the twentieth century appears to be moving from a state of latency to actualization. The nature of this phenomenon and its educational implications are the foci of this chapter.

Another factor which is central to an understanding of the term "community" is the degree to which an individual is aware of his membership in it. A new-born child, for example, does not realize that he is an integral part of a micro-community, the family; the realization of his membership will result from his experiences. Yet the fact that a child is not aware of his membership in a family does not mean that the family does not exist. To illustrate further, a village ne'er-do-well may not know that he belongs to a community and, indeed, the other members of the community may not sense a common bond with him and may wish that he would deposit himself elsewhere. Nevertheless, he *is* a member of the community because he is an inhabitant of that particular geographical location. This point is crucial to an understanding of analysis of the world community beginning on page 142, for, like the village ne'er-do-well, various nationals, because of their ethnocentricity, are not aware of or deny their membership in the world community. The link between the peoples of the world or their sense of common bond which forms the basis of a dynamic world community are shared by some but not all the inhabitants of the globe. The world community exists *de facto* (in fact) but not necessarily *de scientia* (in knowledge).

We may conclude, then, that a community may exist independently of the thought, will, or conscious activity of its members. Such a community is said to be *dormant*. On the other hand, when the individuals who belong to a community are vitally aware of their membership and consciously behave in certain ways because of it, the community is said to be *dynamic*. Within a dynamic community, the individuals behave in certain ways because of their emotional involvement with one another due to their sense of a common bond. To illustrate, passengers on a transcontinental flight are members of a community, that is, they

---

[7] *Ibid.*, p. 3.

share a certain aerographical space. This community is usually dormant, but if a particular event occurs which causes the passengers to be aware of their "shared experience," such as an engine malfunction, the community may become dynamic.

A society differs from a community in that its creation and perpetuation depend upon man's cognitive and volitional activity. A society exists because of an *act* of man, while a community exists because of a *fact which precedes* man's conscious activity. A society includes *consciously established* institutions which have been developed in order to achieve a given goal or goals. It is identified by the institutions within it which regulate human behavior. A society is sustained when its members internalize the goal or goals as desired ends and when its institutions sustain order through the enforcement of laws.

Since a society results from man's conscious efforts to organize his community in order to achieve certain goals, it will not emerge automatically as a community becomes more dynamic. It is also important to note that any community (whether dormant or dynamic) may be the foundation upon which a society may be developed, but the character of the society (dormant or dynamic) will be determined by the nature of the community upon which the society is built. Thus, a community in which the inhabitants seldom interact with one another and feel no sense of common bond, yet have established institutions and laws, may be labeled a "society-dormant community," and a community in which the inhabitants do feel a common bond, do interact with one another, and also have established institutions and laws, the community is said to be a "society-dynamic community."

From the above analysis we can detect four basic subgroupings of social units:

1. *Dormant Community* — a social unit which results from the fact that certain individuals share similar elements, either physical or mental. The individuals *may not* be aware of the elements which bind them together or, if they are aware of them, their membership in the social unit does not significantly affect their conscious behavior.

2. *Dynamic Community* — a social unit which results from the fact that certain individuals share similar elements,

either physical or mental. The individuals *are* aware of these shared elements, and their conscious behavior is affected by their sense of common bond. Their sense of common bond is rooted in the emotions, rather than in the intellect.

3. *Society-Dormant Community* — a social unit which results from human cognitive and volitional activity and from the desire to achieve a goal or goals. This type of community includes institutions which regulate human activities, and it is sustained by law. The individuals within such a unit are affected behaviorally by the institutions, the laws, and the goals; they do not feel a deep emotional attachment to the social group, however.

4. *Society-Dynamic Community* — a social unit which results from human cognitive, volitional, *and emotional* activity and from man's desire to achieve certain goals. It includes institutions which regulate human activities, and it is sustained by law and the loyalty of its members. The behavior of the individuals within such a grouping is affected by the individual's rational acceptance of the goals, institutions, and laws, and their emotional attachment to the group.

In order to understand the nature of the evolving world community from a dormant community into a dynamic community and to analyze the possibility of the creation of a society-dynamic community, we must first look at other social units that profoundly affect most human beings. As Irving Child has lucidly put it,

> The people in a large community are divided into various overlapping groups, each of which has distinctive norms of behavior for its members and relations to the rest of the community. An individual's habits and attitudes are influenced by the character of the groups to which he belongs, and by the relation of these groups to the rest of society.[8]

All human beings, at birth, automatically belong to three social groupings: family, or micro-community, local community, and world community. An individual belongs to the micro-community

[8] Irvin L. Child, *Italian or American* (New Haven, Conn.: Yale University Press, 1943), p. 18.

because of biological factors; he belongs to a local community because of geographical factors; and he is a part of the world community because of his essential similarity to other beings who belong to his species. All three "natural" communities may be dormant or dynamic and may become societies.

THE MICRO-COMMUNITY: THE FAMILY

The family is the most central social unit to which individuals belong at birth. Its structure varies, however, according to cultural factors. The family in an agrarian society may include more than two generations and may be extended to encompass a variety of blood relatives such as aunts and cousins. Although the sense of common bond between the members of a family is generally rooted in a blood relationship, the kinship factor in some families is difficult to trace. Such extended families are generally labeled "clans." In complex industrialized societies, the family is increasingly becoming nuclear in nature — that is, it is composed solely of parents and their children. Regardless of the structure of the family, however, it is generally an integral part of the larger social system and it plays a vital role in the early nurturing process of the young. In the United States, for example, even though the school has assumed a major role in the educational process, the family is still the first socializing agency with which a child has contact.

The importance of the family in all societies rests upon the fact that the child, unlike the offspring of most other animals, is quite defenseless at birth and has a tenuous hold on life for a rather extended period afterwards. He needs a great deal of care and help if he is to overcome the weaknesses imposed by his limited instincts; if he were turned out to fend for himself soon after birth, he would lose his chance to develop into a mature human being — indeed, he would soon die.

The nature of the micro-community, the family, has generally been a dynamic one, as history attests, but the kind of family that exists and the degree to which it is a dynamic community varies widely. In some primitive societies, where almost every individual in the locality is related by blood, the community is extremely dynamic; the family and local community form one social unit. In the earliest primitive societies, the family was a

An evening of family recreation in the parlor rarely occurs in the United States today. Each member seeks his own diversion outside the family unit.

dynamic community. As men began to make laws, as marriage became a regulated and selective process, and as sexual drives became increasingly controlled by human volition, the family became a society. In the early colonial American society, for example, the family was a society-dynamic community.

The American family, like other social units, is undergoing profound changes as a result of the effects of technological advances. Urbanization, the growth of super-corporate business complexes, and the proliferation of social units which demand the loyalty of its members have significantly altered the structure of the family. The normative elements which govern the family are also evolving. For example, the nuclear family in a large urban center today differs radically from the extended families of the early American settlers. Then, too, the functions of the family have changed. Today, for example, the recreational and economic functions have been largely removed from the family and placed within the hands of other social agencies.

The social norms, or "rules of the game," governing behavior within the family also have been changed. The laws of many nations, for example, include provisions for the dissolution of the family. More significantly perhaps, is the growing trend towards removing the family as a center of human interaction. Our age is witnessing the existence of families which have become society-dormant communities. Although the family society continues to exist, the bond between its members frequently does not affect the behavior of its members. When a home becomes a veritable "boarding house," the family is no longer a dynamic community, even though it may remain a society. This phenomenon profoundly affects the larger societies and has become a central problem for educational institutions.

Diverse social doctrines are currently being presented in an attempt to deal with the immense problems created by the changing patterns of family life. Proposals for the creation of quasi-families are being implemented on a limited scale. The kibbutz in Israel and the "adopted grandparent" plan in the United States, by which individuals of advanced age are given an opportunity to adopt children who are deprived of families, are examples of

On an Israeli kibbutz the children live together, separated from their families. The family unit is not broken, however; a special time is set aside each day for the family to be together.

attempts to deal with the dissolution of the family (the legal abolition of a society) and/or the breakdown of dynamic communities
into dormant communities. The breakdown of the family into a
dormant community may be a more crucial phenomenon than the
rate of the legal abolition (divorce) of the family since the family's
central purpose is the emotional development of the young. Since
the emotional element of family is rooted in the community concept, the relevancy of a family that has developed into a dormant
community is questionable.

THE LOCAL COMMUNITY

The local community in which all individuals belong also plays
a significant role in the nurturing process of children. Early in
a child's life, he will learn the norms and behavioral expectations
imposed upon him by his neighbors as well as by his immediate
family. Mandelbaum, who has identified diverse kinds of communities such as hordes, bands, villages, and neighborhoods, writes:

> The essential idea, no matter which particular term is used, is
> that of a group of people, all of whom live within a limited area
> and co-operate to some extent. . . . Because in acting together
> they feel rewarded for so doing, they are ready and willing to
> work together in the future.[9]

Although this description goes beyond the limitations of the term
"community" as utilized in this analysis, it is valuable, for it illustrates how a community often results in the creation of a society. Primarily because of physical proximity, families band together and assume membership within a larger social unit called
a community. As pointed out on page 130, when the inhabitants
of such a grouping consciously set out to achieve certain goals,
societies are developed. Thus, generally, local communities have
become societies.

In the above description, we have another situation in which a
dynamic community becomes the basis for the development of a
society. However, as also mentioned previously, some local societies have developed from dormant communities — for example,

[9] David G. Mandelbaum, "Social Groupings," in *Man, Culture and Society,* ed. Harry L. Shapiro (New York: Oxford University Press, 1964),
p. 288.

the many "pre-fab" suburban communities that have been constructed "overnight" to house workers in a newly developed industrial complex. Although the inhabitants of these communities rarely interact with one another and lack a sense of common bond, they do have institutions and laws. Nevertheless these societies are dormant, and there is often a sense of alienation among the inhabitants.

Sometimes these suburban dwellers will organize groups, such as a Junior League, to revitalize their communities, but such organizations often become ends in themselves because they fail to regenerate the community spirit within the society, even though they may serve to develop a sense of common bond among the members.

What problems are created by the breakdown of local communities into dormant communities? Can the schools assist in revitalizing them? Do the large, comprehensive schools encourage the perpetuation of dormant communities?

Although the alterations in the family and the local community structures in modern industrialized societies present numerous regional and internal problems, they also affect the development of the world community. Social units are often linked together. A dynamic family-community may help to generate a dynamism in the local community. As Edmund Burke commented many years ago, the affection directed to one's "little platoon" may be the "germ" of a love for one's country and for mankind.

It appears that the local community and, to a lesser degree, the family, are moving away from dynamic interaction toward a dormant stage in which meaningful interaction is minimal or lacking altogether. The long-range effects of such a development can hardly be imagined.

THE NATION-STATE

Between the local community and the world community exists a plethora of social groupings, the most significant of which is the nation-state. Although it is not a natural group, the nation-state plays a central role in the lives of most people on earth. Nation-states occupy most land areas of the globe. Not only do they represent the most extended groupings of peoples into societies and communities, but their number has increased markedly during the last twenty years.

Many suburban towns are dormant communities in which
the people live together but do not interact.

n contrast, the Amish
eople today have main-
iained a dynamic com-
iunity. When a house
s being built all the
ien in the town work
gether to complete the
isk.

A nation-state is a *society* because it comes into existence through human action and because it includes a diversity of institutions set up to achieve a desired goal or goals. It is usually a society that has emerged from a foundation of dynamic communities.

Just as physical proximity provides the basis for the existence of a local community, and as relationship of blood provides the foundation for the family, and as the essential similarity between peoples forms the basis of the world community, cultural factors combine with *nationalism* and *patriotism* to form the foundation of the nation-state.

Nationalism is a concept which implies the existence or the desire for the existence of a political, social, and economic unit and which includes the concomitant belief in the development and maintenance of loyalty to that unit. It is nationalism which identifies the nation-state as a society because it brings about the integration of peoples who do not directly interact with one another and who do not possess a "natural" bond. Nationalists, however, have generally attempted to discover elements which form a "natural" bond. Nationality, race, and diverse other factors have been proposed. The continuous process of hybridization of the world's population throughout man's history would appear to negate the existence of such a bond. Beginning with the French Revolution, nationalism has played a central role in the creation and development of nations. Patriotism, the emotional counterpart of nationalism, creates a sense of common bond and makes a nation-state a *community*.

A term which symbolizes the fact that a nation-state is a dynamic community is "fatherland." In the United States the usual phenomenon whereby a dynamic community evolves into a society was reversed. Our nation-state, a *society,* was created by our founding fathers before a dynamic American community came into existence. Perhaps this is what Robert Frost alluded to when he wrote "The land was ours before we were the land's." A dynamic community was soon created, however, which encompassed the political boundaries of the national society, largely through the efforts of the nascent public school system, and before many years had passed, children were joining voices to sing "Columbia, the Gem of the Ocean."

During the historical period when America emerged as a nation-state, its people often reflected the ambivalence that exists when a new society is formed. Some declared themselves Loyalists, thus affirming their loyalty to the *community* labeled "the British Empire," and refused to acknowledge the existence of the newly-formed *society* called "America." Others, believing in the existence of an American society, continued to express a primary loyalty to their regional *communities* (e.g., Virginia).

Later in our national history, the nation-state broke into two distinct *dynamic communities,* the North and the South, and a bloody civil war resulted when an attempt was made to develop a separate *society,* the Confederacy.

The issue of nationalism is central to the educational endeavor, for nationalism is developed through education. As Raymond E. Callahan has asserted, "It is no exaggeration to say that developing citizens loyal to our country is the first concern of the American schools, as it is the first concern of schools in every other nation-state."[10] Nationalism, therefore, is a belief which is necessary for the creation and preservation of the society called a nation-state. A nation-state is a community because of the sense of belonging which is expressed through patriotism. Patriotism makes a society, labeled nation-state, a dynamic community.

The task of teachers in all societies labeled nation-state is to help preserve the *existence* (not necessarily the existing *form*) of the nation-state and to develop in all neophyte citizens an emotional expression of their loyalty in the form of patriotism. We must make clear, however, the fact that nationalism is herein contrasted with *exaggerated nationalism,* which is a belief in the superiority of the nation-state over all other social organizations and, indeed, superior to the individuals who compose it. The emotional counterpart of "exaggerated nationalism" is *chauvinism.*

The fact that nationalism and patriotism easily turn into exaggerated nationalism and chauvinism is sadly exemplified in the history of the twentieth century. Indeed, the two bloody world wars were rooted in a perversion of nationalism and patriotism. This phenomenon has led many individuals to believe that world peace and international order can only be established if nationalism and nation-states are abolished. The issue they raise is of central concern to teachers, for if their claim is true, then teachers,

---

[10] Raymond E. Callahan, *An Introduction to Education in American Society* (New York: Alfred A. Knopf, 1958), pp. 157–158.

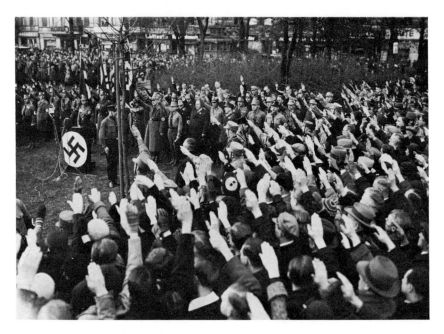

A celebration of Hitler's forty-fourth birthday in Berlin. This period of history illustrates nationalism that became twisted and exaggerated.

if they are to serve mankind, must seek to destroy the very states which they are assigned the task of preserving.

This pertinent issue will be examined in the next section. Now let us ponder the question of whether a nation-state which is based upon exaggerated nationalism and sustained by the loyalty of its people through chauvinism, such as Nazi Germany, can continue to be a society. A society is based upon the intellect and will of man. Can the mental aberration of exaggerated nationalism and the blinding emotional disease, chauvinism, exist concomitantly with reason and freedom of will? A society exists to achieve a certain goal or goals which are separate from the society. When exaggerated nationalism prevails, a society becomes an end in itself.

NATIONALISM AND INTERNATIONALISM

Internationalism or world-mindedness, if placed in opposition to nationalism results in a false dichotomy. In fact, the existence of international cooperation and the hope of the development of an eventual world society rests upon the existence of nation-states. If there were no nation-states, who would represent the diverse peoples of the world in international conferences or in a world government? What political sub-unit would form the basis for cooperative efforts? If nation-states were abolished, would a world congress, for example, be composed of representatives from every city, village, state, hamlet, or tribe in the world?

Some may argue that the political subdivisions of such a union, rather than being the present nation-states, could be religious, racial, or cultural units. Assuming that either one of these alternatives were utilized, wouldn't that particular grouping, when provided with a *political* organization, become in fact a nation-state? Besides, such a choice is not really available to us, for racial, religious, and cultural groupings do not exist in clearly defined segments, as Kluckhohn has noted:

> With some qualifications and exceptions, one may say that, if all living people were ranged in a single sequence according to degree of resemblance, there would be no sharp breaks in the line but rather a continuum where each specimen differed from the next by almost imperceptible variations.[11]

Although Kluckhohn is referring to racial characteristics only, the same statement may be applied to cultures, because of the continuous process of cultural diffusion, and to religion because of ecumenism. Indeed, religious and cultural groupings have become as difficult to distinguish as racial characteristics in our hybrid world population.

The key issue teachers face is not whether they should teach about nation-states in order to develop national loyalty, or teach the abolition of the nation-state in order to develop world-mindedness. The issue is how to discover the "happy mean" between nationalism and internationalism and between patriotism and world-mindedness. As in the case of the need to preserve a person's individualism while assimilating him into a society, discussed

[11] Clyde Kluckhohn, *Mirror for Man* (New York: Fawcett World Library, 1965), p. 105.

in Chapter 5, the problem is how to strike the proper balance between national individualism and assimilation into the world community. When nations are not assimilated into the world community, anarchy often results. The devastation that resulted from
the World Wars (the twentieth century's Thirty Years War) provides us with a vivid reminder of the consequences of international
anarchy. Yet, if nations lose their identity, the resultant sameness
would be paralyzing. The great artists, musicians, and literary
geniuses of the world have produced their "works of art" within
cultural settings. The differences between Spanish and German
music, for example, illustrate that culture is a vital source of creative genius. The elimination of cultural differences which are
often preserved and enhanced by nation-states would result in the
destruction of a vital wellspring of creativity. As mentioned in
Chapter Five, cultural pluralism *within* a nation-state is difficult to
preserve. The foundation of world order rests upon the preservation of nation-states within a community or society of nations.

THE WORLD COMMUNITY AND THE EMERGING WORLD SOCIETY

The world community is a fact which precedes man's activity.
It exists because of the oneness of the human species. It becomes
a dynamic community when men sense the bond which unites
them and when their conscious behavior reflects their awareness
of and their emotional attachment to the community.

Man's awareness of his position as an integral member of a
world community depends upon his speculative capacity to see
beyond the non-essential differences which distinguish him from
other humans. Indeed, the language of primitive peoples often
refers to themselves as "the people" while describing foreigners
in diverse derogatory terms. The Slavs, for example, referred to
the Germans as the *niemci,* which means "the mutes."

Although meaningful interaction with the "others" who belong
to the outside group is a usual stepping stone to the development
of a bond between peoples, some rare human beings throughout
man's recorded history were able to feel their brotherhood with
all human beings without first having interacted with them.
These compassionate philosophers, because of their affective and

cognitive genius, were able to feel without direct empirical evidence that the ecstasy and sorrows which they carried within their own hearts were carried within the heart of humanity.

From these great mystics, such as Jesus and Buddha, came a vital spark which began the process of making dynamic the world community — a process which has continued to the present time. Unlike the family and the local community, the world community has changed from a dormant community to a dynamic community, and is ripe for the creation of a world society. In the rest of this section we will identify some of the recent developments that have brought about the development of a dynamic world community and isolate some of the twentieth-century characteristics of the emerging world society.

Recent technological developments have necessitated that man, at least psychologically, achieve a rapprochement with his fellow human beings. The technological advances in communication and transportation, and the economic needs of industrial societies, have brought us all closer together. In an age when we can travel at a rate in excess of 1,600 miles per hour, and when mass media instantaneously relate events from throughout the globe, the shrill of an ambulance siren in Saigon produces the same tensions as a siren in one's own neighborhood. Indeed, our world has become our neighborhood, and all our fellow creatures have become our family.

The explosion of a crude atomic bomb near Alamogordo, New Mexico, on July 16, 1945 (a date which in history courses continues to play second fiddle to 1066) has not only revolutionized our potential application of energy but also has changed our concept of survival. The pre-atomic concepts of "the survival of the fittest" and "just wars" have been increasingly questioned. In this age of super-power, the decisions of two or three nations to assume a warring stance with one another encompass all the peoples of the world. Whether the new developments in technology will produce a new code of ethics in our lifetime remains to be seen; what is certain, however, is that a global war today may not only be fatal to the warring factions but may result in the genocide of the human race. The choice is no longer between "my ideology or my death," but rather between "my ideology or mankind's death." Today the world is avoiding a conflagration in great measure because of fear. We are living in the age of the *pax atomica*, and because of it, my fear is your fear and our fear is mankind's fear.

We do not only share our fears but also our joys and our sorrows. A great technological feat, a great breakthrough in medicine, produces joy throughout the world. And when a young president is assassinated or a daring young cosmonaut dies in a frightful plunge to earth, everyone weeps together.

The development of large industrial societies has not only resulted in the extension of social units into the largest integrated groupings ever witnessed upon the earth, but it also has given rise

Foreign dignitaries leave the White House to walk behind John F. Kennedy's funeral caisson enroute to St. Matthew's Cathedral. Assembled here are heads of state from West Germany, France, Greece, Belgium, Ethiopia, the Philippines, and Korea.

to universal education, cultural homogenization, and *ideological* foundations for nationalism and patriotism.

Because of the need for a literate population to sustain an industrial society, with all its intricate social institutions, universal education has become a goal of nearly all the nation-states on earth. And with the growth of education, ideologies have become a central force in the struggle to preserve and sustain nationalism and patriotism. Industrialism, however, results in changes in institutions and eventually in the values upon which a society rests, and we are now witnessing an alteration of values on an unprecedented scale. The current struggle over birth control brought about because of medical advances (both in the ability to control birth and to preserve life and, thus, producing a "population explosion") symbolizes the conflict between emerging values and traditional ones.

The great mass societies are also being forced to alter their ideologies in order to cope with the changing social situations that have arisen because of technology, and the emerging values, since they too result in great measure because of the factor of technology, will tend to bring ideologies closer together. Thus, dichotomous ideologies may, in time, become less dichotomous. For example, the "grass-roots democracy" of the United States and the "centralized democracy" of the Soviet Union are continuously being altered in the face of technological and social realities. Whether such changes *should* alter values is a relevant question; however, barring the construction of another China-like "Great Wall" or a rejection on a large scale of technological advances, the ideological convergence will take place.

As contacts between nations continue and as economic interdependence develops further, the phenomenon of cultural diffusion will eliminate some of the sharp edges from the differences between cultures.

Another phenomenon which results from the complex interaction and interdependence of modern nation-states is the gradual elimination of reasonable alternatives to internationalism.

The reason usually given for rejecting an international cooperative world order is to preserve the nation's "way of life." But is this really possible? Can a nation preserve its way of life by rejecting international cooperation? In order to answer that question, the alternatives to international cooperation must be identified.

The alternatives to international cooperation are (1) isolation, (2) imperialism, (3) cold war, and (4) hot war. Isolation or the closing off of national boundaries in order to preserve a nation's way of life, would in fact produce the opposite effect. Not only would such a phenomenon be quite impossible for the United States in this age of relatively inexpensive world travel and powerful communication systems, but it would jeopardize the very freedoms that are central to our way of life. It would also drastically alter our present economic system, which rests to a great degree upon international trade. Cultural diffusion is unavoidable in our present world situation; our technology has made isolation not only impractical but virtually impossible.

The second alternative, imperialism, is equally obsolete. In addition, if utilized by the United States, it would violate the basic tenets of our way of life and, thus, would serve to destroy it rather than preserve it.

The third alternative, cold war, or a struggle between two nations or among many nations on a massive international scale in order to preserve a balance of world power, is not an alternative at all, for it implies a certain amount of international cooperation in order to keep the cold war from becoming a hot war. And the fourth alternative, hot war can be even more easily dismissed because of the terrible consequences mentioned previously.

Needless to say, the degree to which a nation involves itself internationally and with whom is a variable within internationalism. The form of international involvement will depend upon the nature of the "happy mean" between nationalism and internationalism. The diverse political and social pressures placed upon the schools and other institutions in American society would seem to indicate that the happy mean has not as yet been discovered. However, one cannot avoid noting that at the present time, the world community is continuing to emerge.

The forces and characteristics of the world community discussed above indicate that the world is in a nascent stage of a developing society. Perhaps a basic form for the emerging world society is currently taking shape as various nation-states begin to structure institutions to regulate their international business activities. The Common Market in Europe, for example, resembles the early stages of the confederation formed by the American colonies before the ratification of the Constitution. The United Nations, although its regulations cannot be enforced and although its executive, legislative, and judicial powers are limited, may be the seed from which a world society will emerge.

Education for World Citizenship

The chances of such a society developing will depend ultimately upon the dynamism of the world community and the willingness of the peoples of the world to relinquish some of the powers now held by nations. Whether this will be accomplished in our lifetime will depend ultimately upon education. It will be within the schools that the blindness of ethnocentrism will be removed. The school must also ensure that the perceptions developed within an individual's "specific behavioral world" will not inhibit the progress toward a world society.

The sense of unity among the peoples of the world can, like nationalism and patriotism, be instilled into the minds and hearts of young people. Although the modern world with its trans-world communication and rapid transportation has brought about an awareness of the existence of a world community, the school must play a central role in sustaining the emerging dynamic world community. As Bertrand Russell says,

> If there is to be effective international cooperation, such as was hoped for by the creators of the League of Nations and the United Nations, there will have to be very widespread education of an internationalist character.[12]

The school must also prepare children for citizenship in a world society.

THE CONTROL OF EDUCATION

Since most social groupings into which children are born and nurtured assume the task of socializing them so that they will "fit"

[12] Bertrand Russell in *The Basic Writings of Bertrand Russell*, eds. Robert E. Egner and Lester E. Denonn (New York: Simon and Schuster, 1961), p. 707.

within the group, children, all of whom resemble one another more than they resemble adults, soon become mirrors of specific cultures. The plasticity of human beings is what leads to the great diversity of characteristics which are internalized within a social setting.

Parents nurture their children so that they will behave according to the familiar established norms. Local agencies, including the formal educational system as well as informal educational organizations (e.g., a local historical society) play a central role in the socialization process, guiding the child so that he will fit into his community.

The public school also plays a central role in the assimilation of individuals into the nation-state. In some nations, such as France, where education is under the direct control of a centralized national agency, the process is direct and the norms and behavioral expectations are set and disseminated to local agencies. In the United States, however, where the educational endeavor is in the hands of local and state agencies, the norms and expectations concerning national citizenship are significantly similar throughout the land and result from frequent and intense communication and consensus. For example, every public school system in the United States requires that all secondary school children learn the history of the Republic, and many other organizations, ranging from the Boy Scouts to the Daughters of the American Revolution, assist the schools in this process.

The pressure which non-educational agencies can bring to bear upon the schools depends upon internal and international conditions. During periods of internal unrest and/or international disorder, the pressure to instill loyalty in youth is increased. Unless teachers courageously and critically analyze such pressures, exaggerated nationalism, or chauvinism, will reach into the classroom.

The world community, not being a society, possesses few educational agencies, and those it does have, such as UNESCO, serve primarily in advisory capacities. Therefore, it cannot control or direct the process of assimilating individuals into the world community. The process of assimilating individuals into a world society, and the degree to which it will be attempted, rests completely upon the willingness of nation-states and their educational representatives to implement such a goal.

Teachers within the diverse nation-states bear the responsibility for developing world-mindedness, and at the present time, the hope for the establishment of a world society rests almost entirely in their hands. Carleton Washburne puts it this way:

> . . . the schools and colleges are the one agency which consistently, day in and day out, year in and year .out, in a coordinated and organized way, can consciously and directly affect the understanding, behavior, and attitudes of all those who will compose the world of tomorrow.[13]

THE FUNCTION OF THE SCHOOL

If it is assumed that assimilation into the world community is of central importance in the educational endeavor, certain primary factors are crucial to teachers and education.

The experiences within the school must enable the students to learn about the characteristics and development of various institutions within diverse societies. Such experiences should assist students in the process of analytically viewing the similarities and differences among world cultures, the ultimate aim of which would be to affect students' attitudes in order to enable them to view the ever-changing world scene objectively. The aim, therefore, is to develop attitudes that reflect the unity of mankind. Knowledge *of* the development of various cultures will not suffice, and is not, *per se,* the end of education for world understanding. The needs of the modern world demand that our students feel, think, and act with openmindedness and with an open heart:

> Cultural empathy enables a person to see other nations and his own in true perspective. He can perceive both similarities and differences between cultures, he can see the relationships among cultural, political, economic, and educational factors; he can recognize national characteristics but avoid national stereotypes.[14]

---

[13] Carleton Washburne, *The World's Good* (New York: John Day Company, 1954), p. x.

[14] National Education Association, Project on Instruction, *Education in a Changing Society* (Washington: The Association, 1963), p. 108.

Education to develop cultural empathy would necessitate an understanding of the various patterns of human expression in diverse cultures. By experiencing many different realms of human expression, students will begin to understand the total meaning of the culture of another society. Too often we find adults who cannot, for example, see meaning in oriental art or Middle Eastern symbolism. Education in comparative culture and the multifaceted meanings therein could provide a beginning of this kind of understanding for students. Such a beginning would contribute to the students' awareness of the diversity of ways of expressing meaning and lead to the desired establishment of empathy. It would also lead to a greater appreciation of our own expression of meaning. The responsibility for the development of programs reflecting this view is, therefore, not exclusively a task for the social studies teacher but, rather, is the task of all those who teach. According to the report of a conference which inaugurated a program to improve the teaching of world affairs in Glens Falls, New York, the desired experiences are to be derived from "art, biology, business education, foreign language, homemaking, industrial arts, mathematics, music and physical education as well as in social studies and English language arts."

Several years ago the Educational Policies Commission of the National Education Association asserted that the central purpose of the school was to develop the ability to think. This goal is consistent with the goal of developing empathy for all peoples in all societies, for empathy is rooted in reason as well as in emotion. A concomitant goal is the development of a critical mind. Mumford says, "No habit must be uncriticized; no values must remain unexamined; no institutional procedures must be regarded as sacred; no life-denying goals must remain unchallenged."[15]

The Birth of a World Society

The aim of developing a world community is also based upon an understanding of oneself. Perception is selective and the nature of the selectivity depends not only upon one's culture but also upon one's self-concept. What is the relationship between an

[15] Mumford, *op. cit.*, p. 257.

individual's self-concept and his perception of others? To what extent do family and local community interrelationships affect an individual's disposition to develop empathy for the other members of the world community? How do we re-educate an individual who is snared by cultural self-centeredness?

Empathy, like charity, begins at home. It is extremely doubtful that any people, wherever they may be and whoever they may be, who cannot resolve differences peacefully within their own homes, communities, regions, or nations will ever be able to develop a sense of communion with peoples of foreign lands. One of the saddest, indeed most pathetic occurrences of this modern world is the call for world peace by spokesmen for nations who cannot live at peace with their own neighbors or even with themselves. World peace must begin in the human heart, for only communities or societies who have found peace among themselves will be able to take the necessary step toward world peace advocated in the following optimistic message from Martin Buber:

> I believe, despite all, that the peoples in this hour can enter into dialogue, into a genuine dialogue with one another. In a genuine dialogue each of the partners, even when he stands in opposition to the other, heeds, affirms, and confirms his opponent as an existing other.[16]

As we witness the birth of a world society, we must discover what the evolving nature of that society is and what will be needed to sustain it. When all factors are considered, such as time available, readiness, the nature of man's accumulated knowledge, the central goals of the school must flow from the needs of the individual and the needs of society, for it is for them that we exist and in them that our hopes rest.

The following words of Dag Hammarskjold provide a fitting conclusion to this chapter:

> . . . [Jesus] sat at meat with publicans and sinners, he consorted with harlots. Did he do this to obtain their votes? Or did he think that, perhaps, he could convert them by such "ap-

[16] Martin Buber, *Pointing the Way* (New York: Harper & Row, 1963), p. 238.

peasement"? Or was his humanity rich and deep enough to make contact, even in them, with that in human nature which is common to all men, indestructible, and upon which the future has to be built?[17]

SUGGESTIONS FOR FURTHER READING

Arieli, Yehoshua. *Individualism and Nationalism in American Ideology.* Baltimore: Penguin Books, 1964.

DeChardin, Pierre Teilhard. *The Future of Man.* New York: Harper & Row, 1964.

Everett, Samuel (ed.). *Teaching World Affairs in American Schools.* New York: Harper & Brothers, 1956.

Horowitz, Irving Louis. *Three Worlds of Development: The Theory and Practice of International Stratification.* New York: Oxford University Press, 1966.

Jaspers, Karl. *The Future of Mankind.* Chicago: The University of Chicago Press, 1961.

Jensen, Merrill (ed.). *Regionalism in America.* Madison: The University of Wisconsin Press, 1965.

Kenworthy, Leonard S. *Introducing Children to the World.* New York: Harper & Brothers, 1956.

King, Edmund J. *World Perspectives in Education.* New York: The Bobbs-Merrill Company, 1962.

Van Dyke, Vernon. *International Politics.* New York: Appleton-Century-Crofts, 1966.

Wiggin, Gladys A. *Education and Nationalism: An Historical Interpretation of American Education.* New York: McGraw-Hill Book Co., 1962.

---

[17] Dag Hammarskjold, *Markings* (New York: Alfred A. Knopf, 1965), p. 157.

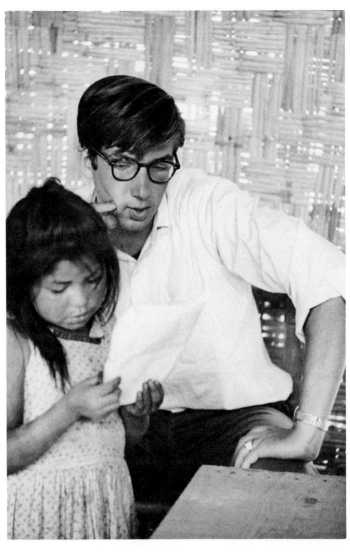

Chimbote, Peru: Instruction in a small school constructed of bamboo matting.

Chapter Seven

THE VALUING
PROCESS IN EDUCATION

Values are what people hold in high esteem, the objects and instruments, the experiences and relationships, the qualities, conditions, and objectives men prize as worthy of human effort and interest. Valuing is a common human experience necessary to every reasonable, goal-directed life and to every stable, productive society.

To develop and clarify the concept of value and the human experience of valuing leads to controversies which have both challenged and plagued the best minds for centuries. These controversies and the value theories by which their resolution is proposed are intimately entwined with the social processes of education.

The schools, their students, teachers, administrators, and supporting personnel eventually face the perplexing but intriguing problem of defining the nature of values, and the nature of man himself and his society. Just how do values come to operate legitimately and authoritatively in ordering human affairs?

Does the quality of value reside in the object of value itself? Is an object of value prized because of its own inherent character or possession? Or does the object of value *become* valuable when we need or desire it for what we believe to be a better life? The

question of whether value is *intrinsic,* residing in the objects themselves, or *instrumental,* a means of attaining additional values, is
significant in many ways to the educator. For example, is knowledge an intrinsic value, a value in and of and for itself, or is
the value of knowledge contingent upon its application in human
experience? Is education a value per se, or does its value rest, at
least in part, in the experiences and attainments it brings within
human grasp? Answers to these questions influence both the
methods and aims of education as well as the curriculum. What
we teach, how we teach it, and why, are essentially questions
about values.

The Sources of Values

COSMIC VS. INDIVIDUAL VALUES

Even more demanding questions regarding values confront the
professional teacher for whom teaching is more than a mere craft.
As both an art and a science, teaching poses the question of the
sources of values. Do the values we esteem grow out of individual,
subjective tastes and desires? If so, are our human passions in-
herently evil, good, or amoral?

Obviously, an educational system based on the assumption that
individuals choose their values because of depraved impulses will
differ considerably from one which is operated on the premise that
human beings are innately moral. Proponents of the former system, history indicates, tend to emphasize the process of formation,
in which knowledge and values are pressed in from without, as if
external forces were needed to control the evil impulses within.
Strong discipline, in the form of authoritarian indoctrination and
prescribed values, including moral dogmas and fixed subject matter, characterizes this kind of educational system.

Those who uphold the other kind of system — that in which
learning experiences are organized on a basis of the legitimacy of
subjective values derived from inner desires which are considered
naturally good — think that educational experiences should be
far more relaxed, less demanding. They believe that the motivation for learning comes from within, that education is a matter of
realizing one's inner potential, rather than adjusting to the demands of an external reality. This type of education has been

criticized as being so individualistic that it leads to a freedom bordering on anarchy which thwarts the development of social perspectives.

These two extremes in educational philosophy — the theory of adjustment to the "external" world and that of the realization of one's "internal" world, or self-realization — have existed throughout most of the history of educational theory and practice and are still accepted and defended by many. Yet neither meets the demands of contemporary thought, which denies the need for a division of reality into the objective external and the subjective internal. This denial of the ultimate separation of the individual and his sociophysical environment leads to further value controversies which, as we shall see, have revolutionized our concepts of learning and valuing.

For many, values cannot be determined by the fluctuating, whimsical desires of isolated individuals. What we rightly esteem is not a matter of human decision or desire. Rather, values are assigned to us from some extra-historical source for cosmic rather than individual reasons. Thus, according to this view, values are eternal, immutable, irrevocable, and necessary, for we are a certain kind of being, living in a certain kind of reality and working out the inevitable purposes commissioned to us.

If human values are thus *prescribed,* the task of the school, and every other social institution, is clear and distinct. The aim of education is to transmit these absolute values and see that they are accepted by young people. The moral standards, values, and principles of the good life are passed on without question and without teaching the learner how to deal with value conflicts or how to evaluate and justify his own norms and goals.

Historically, the schools of both Europe and America, both secular and religious, both public and private, have served their broader societies in this passive role. Learning has been viewed primarily as the passive reception by the student of knowledge, facts, skills, and values. The cultural heritage, organized into distinct subject matters and embodying fixed, absolute values, defines the content of the curriculum. Whenever prescribed, cosmic values set the aims of education, individual desires, and the processes of human development and the practical needs of society have been of little concern.

For some contemporary teachers, the basic function of the

school continues to be to deliver to the student absolute values received from some extra-human source and incorporated into tradition. But the absolutist faces the unnerving problem of deciding which of the multiple systems of absolute values, each claiming unending, universal authority, is the right one, for only a single set of eternal, absolute values is logically possible. The fact that men have often vied with one another, even to the point of violence, over the merits of mutually exclusive systems of absolute values suggests the strong possibility that values are, after all, in some way a matter of human choice and social derivation.

This argument does not, of course, refute the existence of absolute values. (Only an absolute theory can reject the existence of absolutes — an obvious logical absurdity.) But the fact that men have been incapable of reconciling their conflicting absolutes indicates that there is very little possibility of basing a democratic system of education in a pluralistic society on absolute values. The notion is, indeed, a contradiction in terms.

The traditionalists, who justify the transmission of an unmodified cultural heritage on the ground that whatever is traditional is also valuable, face a similar problem. The fact of the matter is that there is no single cultural heritage, no tradition *qua* tradition. There are many cultural traditions, most of which conflict with themselves as much as with one another. When a teacher, therefore, advocates traditional values by appealing to tradition alone, what he has actually done is to choose some particular values and practices from within some specific tradition. And these selections, like all value judgments, are debatable.[1]

EXPERIENCE AS A SOURCE OF VALUES

There is a third possible source of values other than the individual and the cosmic. The successful application of the scientific method to human affairs and social problems supports the notion that values need not be a matter of individual tastes or cosmic absolutes but are human constructs built up through social experience by men for the purpose of insuring the survival of their society and enhancing the quality of human existence. In other

[1] Harold Weisberg, "Tradition and the Traditionalist," in *Philosophy and Education,* 2nd ed., ed. Israel Scheffler (Boston: Allyn and Bacon, 1966), p. 356.

words, by rational, objective methods of discovery and problem solving, men are capable of defining, evaluating, and revising their social and moral norms and the objectives of human history.

Accordingly, the teacher need not appeal to either undemonstrable absolutes or tradition in fulfilling education's passive role of transmitting a static cultural heritage. The schools will no doubt continue to contribute to the stability and continuity of society by transmitting values of the past. But this traditional, passive role of the school is being increasingly matched by the active role of social innovation.[2]

As research produces new skills and knowledge, as greater numbers of people acquire more tolerant and liberal attitudes through education, as the classroom increases its influence in determining economic status, the school becomes more active in its influence upon society, its institutions, interests, and values. It is in this role of modifying cultural values and changing social interests and institutions that the school faces its greatest challenge and its gravest problem.

Increasing numbers of educators, statesmen, sociologists, and philosophers are claiming that, for the sake of a society undergoing massive expansion in multiple directions, the schools must meet this challenge. This need not mean, however, that the schools would control the direction of social change. Many social agencies and institutions other than the schools have the same democratic prerogative of influencing new ways of organizing social experience. It is rather the case that the schools would take the lead, without neglecting their traditional passive role of serving the needs of society, in developing minds which are capable of dealing with novel situations that affect all kinds of social, economic, political, and religious institutions.

Nor does this active role grant the schools and the teachers a mandate to define and transmit a new system of cultural values. Such a system, would of course, be authoritarian and artificial. The values of a genuinely democratic society will be gradually defined and redefined through the practical experiences of the masses in the light of many diversified interests and needs. The innovating role of the school, then, is not to supply new values, but to

[2] Burton Clark, *Educating the Expert Society* (San Francisco: Chandler Publishing Co., 1962), Chapter 1.

prepare youthful minds to undertake the cooperative tasks of recognizing value conflicts, identifying their causes and conditions, and applying rational methods of value re-organization.

THE EVALUATION OF VALUES: PRAGMATISM AND EXPERIMENTALISM IN AMERICA

Before the schools or any other social institution can undertake the active role of social innovation through the critical evaluation of values, it must have a guiding philosophy of education. This philosophy will have to be capable of directing large-scale human efforts in constantly reconstructing the values of society and the objectives of history. It must also be able to gain the widespread support of great masses of people who can intelligently and cooperatively engage in the process of re-evaluating the bases and goals of their social experiences. Needless to say, such a theory of active social reconstruction would itself be constantly subject to criticism and revision.

Growing out of the only distinctively American philosophy, Pragmatism, such an educational philosophy has gradually emerged. In the late nineteenth century Charles Sanders Peirce, founder of Pragmatism, asserted that the meaning of an idea rested solely on the consequences of the action which put that idea to work. In other words, an idea has no meaning prior to or apart from experience. Theory and practice are, therefore, interactive and mutually dependent. The same pragmatic relationship exists, as we shall see later, between means and ends.

The experimental attitude toward values and morals which grew out of this pragmatic theory of meaning subjects judgments about value to tests according to objective data evolving from behavior based on such judgments. Value judgments are not mere expressions of individual tastes that are neither true nor false, neither right nor wrong. Thus the practice of education aims at developing intelligence which is growing in the capacity to distinguish what is liked and what is likable, what is satisfying and what is satisfactory, what is desired and what is desirable.

In fine, the old and universal practice of deliberate education recognizes the pervasive role of impulse and desire in human conduct, but it is also grounded in the assumption that there is a significant and irreducible difference between behavior dominated and blinded by the urgent appeal of some immediate desire, and behavior that is consciously governed by consideration of associated and long-run consequences.[3]

The experimentalist, therefore, puts a greater emphasis on the processes of valuing and re-evaluating than on the transmission of values — no matter how deeply engrained in the cultural heritage a given value may be. This emphasis on the methods of making value decisions and testing those decisions by the consequences of action makes no appeal to absolutes. Values are never conceived as ultimate ends in themselves but as *ends in view* which, when attained, serve as instrumental *means* to still other ends in view.

End-Values and Mean-Values

VALUES IN THE PRESCIENTIFIC WORLD

For the greater part of the history of Western culture men have reasoned that ends and the means to those ends were separate and distinct. Accordingly, the *ends,* or goals, of human experience were considered to be intrinsic values, or values, as we have seen, which are ends in themselves, requiring no justification beyond their absolute existence. *Means,* on the other hand, were esteemed for their extrinsic value in providing for the attainment of ends. Obviously, the validity of mean-values was contingent upon the validity of end-values. The way men ordered their experiences and directed their lives could be justified only by appealing to the ends which defined the meaning and purpose of experience.

Thus, in the prescientific era, before men began to rely on practical methods of testing their judgments of value goals, the meaning and purpose of human experience was generally considered to be assigned by cosmic decree beyond human ratification. Human judgments based on experience carried little or no authoritative appeal in a world characterized by suspicion and superstition. Therefore, men gave weight to the beliefs and value judgments that were gleaned from practical, social experiences by incorporating them, no doubt unconsciously, into their authoritative myths and sacred writings. The secular, the consequences of

[3] John L. Childs, *American Pragmatism and Education* (New York: Henry Holt & Co., 1956), p. 120.

human endeavor, the socially derived truths and values, were void of objectivity, for man had not yet envisioned the methods of directing his own destiny.

Greek tragedy is a case in point. The inevitable, irrevocable end toward which life ran its inexorable course was by far to be more prized than the fleeting pleasures to be gained by taking one's destiny into one's own hands and directing the course of one's life according to subjective individual tastes. These were the only two alternatives envisioned by pre-scientific societies: to find order in necessary ends and absolute values which transcend the scope of time and space, on the one hand, or, on the other, to resign oneself to the chaos and anarchy of individual whim. Even the experimentalist, who now recognizes the further alternative of directing social experience and deriving cultural values through objective, scientific means, would probably agree that, given this limited scope, our ancestors in the ancient and medieval worlds took the better of the two routes open to them.

But the notion of absolute end-values thwarted the realization that human experience is an open-ended affair, subject to redirection by human endeavor. Plato saw every human psyche as the possessor of eternal and unchanging ideals which the pre-existent and eternal human soul brought into the physical world of things (which were unreal copies) from a separate world of real ideas. But no matter how enduring this soul, it could not define its own purposes or values by choice, reason, or even chance. Nor was Plato the only ancient willing to trade freedom for immortality.

Another example of the resignation to prescribed values and the separation of means and ends is Aristotle's view of the good life. Aristotle found the highest human good in that well-being or happiness derived from the use of natural reason. For every fixed form of reality there is an inherent purpose which distinguishes that form from all others. Man's distinctive mark, according to Aristotle, is his rationality; his purpose, contemplative thought.

According to this notion, which has embedded itself deeply within Western thought, the powers of reason do not encompass the *means of defining the aims* of human experience. The meaning and purpose of life are given, and though these gifts of nature may be *discovered* through reason, only the practical means of realizing aims can be *devised* by human thought.

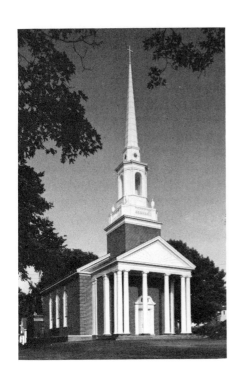

Religious values that once seemed eternal to our society are now being questioned. Recently Dr. Cox, a Harvard University School of Divinity professor, organized "An Evening with God" in an attempt to create a meaningful contemporary religious experience. People of all ages and beliefs came and shared. The program ranged from folk songs by Judy Collins to an illustrated talk by Sister Corita about her graphics work.

The belief in divine revelation also gave value directions to the men of the prescientific world in which ends and means were considered to be independent of each other. Human value goals were thought to be in the hands of God and incapable of being changed by social practice. By the fifth century Augustine, Bishop of Hippo, had denied even the possibility that men could teach and learn true values from one another, much less construct their own values through experience.[4]

Although the value directives of divine revelation were not viewed as socially defined (they would have lost their objectivity and accompanying authority had they been), they increasingly required institutional interpretation, human application, and social systematizing as evolving techno-democratic aspirations afforded ever-widening and increasing social alternatives. In due course, the authority of revelation passed from its divine source to its inspired, though humanly written, literature, to its ecclesiastical institutions. It was only a matter of time until increasing numbers of men realized that there was more of the human than the divine in the revelations.

VALUES IN A PLURALISTIC SOCIETY

Flexibility, Re-Evaluation, and Reorganization. A pluralistic society is first and foremost flexible. It is deliberately organized and reorganized to accomplish specific, changing social purposes rather than to direct the total society toward pre-determined and ultimate ends or to order the entire life of the individual within that society. Accordingly, no pluralistic society or liberal institution within such a society, whether religious, political, economic, or educational, can make any claims to ultimacy or finality. All actions, organizations, and aims are relative to the specific needs of the society from time to time in the light of changing conditions. The society is constantly open to re-evaluation and to reorganization. The educational institutions of the pluralistic society, insofar as they share the broader society's flexibility, participate with other social institutions and organized interest groups in remaking themselves and their society and in reshaping the society's goals and interests.

[4] Aurelius Augustine, *Concerning the Teacher* (New York: Appleton-Century-Crofts, 1938), pp. 46–48.

A pluralistic society is characterized by a multitude of values which are derived from a number of sources by several methods involving a large portion of the population. Because of the massive number of both values and their sources, it should not be surprising that a pluralistic society also faces considerable controversy and conflict over the values of its citizens. Thus, a pluralistic society must incorporate among its social operations some generally accepted means of resolving these disagreements without dogmatically or arbitrarily excluding conflicting values and beliefs. In other words, a pluralistic society is a cooperative human venture based on a common consensus regarding practical means rather than absolute ends.

The traditional definition of "society" as a group of people bound together by common beliefs, purposes, and values does not hold for the pluralistic society. The constituents of a pluralistic society are held together, not by a single set of values, fixed purposes, or an inflexible moral code, but by the several social means and institutions they have created in order to express various interests and achieve differing aims in a variety of ways. It is based on the assumption that social developments can and must take place through a multiplicity of social processes which are humanly defined through social experience, not predetermined by historical inevitability or cosmic necessity.

A pluralistic society, then, is defined and characterized by the quality as well as the quantity of its social processes. These social processes and the educative means which they incorporate are flexible and tentative, never indurated, never beyond re-evaluation and revision. As the goals and values of a pluralistic society must be constantly open to innovation and modification, so too must the social means of achieving these objectives and realizing these values remain compliant to the novel demands of human experience.

Thus, the ends and means of a pluralistic society are interdependent and interactive. A change in the aims of human experience requires a corresponding innovation in the methods directed toward those aims. The values achieved are therefore qualified by the means utilized in defining and deriving social goals. Furthermore, values are never ends in themselves, existing only because of their own intrinsic worth. In a pluralistic society, values are prized for their instrumental character, their appropriateness as means to other, higher values which are conceived by the society in its efforts to improve social experience, to reduce human suffering, and generally to control the course of history.

Education in a Pluralistic Society. The processes of education in a pluralistic society are carried on under the assumption that human intelligence can remake social conditions by solving genuine human problems objectively. Beyond this direction the aims of education in a pluralistic society remain flexible and subject to constant reassessment.

While conserving and using traditional beliefs, values, and institutions as instruments of and bases for innovation, the pluralistic society constantly reassesses these same sources of stability and direction. Tentative values which today direct the reshaping of tomorrow's values may themselves be reorganized by those very values whose creation they are now directing. Conservative interests are valuable to an open society, then, but for the sake of what is being created rather than for what is being conserved.

The schools of such a flexible society make their contributions in these two complementary directions of *conservation* and *creation.* Because the pluralistic society is flexible and therefore is constantly redirecting its efforts toward novel situations and values, the traditional cultural role of education in transmitting and conserving the cultural heritage is more pertinent in the innovative society than it is in the highly ordered primitive societies, absolute monarchies, and police states. The ordered societies require the schools as cultural agents to implant in the maturing generation an unquestioning loyalty to the existing realities. Individuals are expected to adjust to the demands of the current social situations without any special help. Schools serve the society and contribute to its on-going stability by enabling the students to learn what is expected of them in the way of conformity and obedience and by helping them make adjustments to external social demands.

Schools in the open society also transmit the culture's heritage, but the traditional knowledge, beliefs, and values are not presented as possessing unquestionable authority; they serve rather to open the doors to an expanding, evolving future. Education in a flexible society, then, by transmitting the cultural traditions to the maturing youth, helps to insure the foundations of innovation.

The widely divergent uses of the past made by the ordered and planned society, on the one hand, and the open and planning society, on the other, indicate equally conflicting attitudes toward the nature and purpose of the cultural heritage. For the former the cultural heritage is composed of highly organized, logically systematized subject-matter bodies of knowledge. More often than not the rationale or categories of organization are viewed as fixed and necessary, defined outside the realm of human society and prior to human experience. Thus, history, mathematics, language, and other bodies of knowledge are separate and distinct, standing apart within their own consistencies. The cultural role of the school is to transmit these truths, and the student's role is to gratefully receive the wisdom which is imparted to him.

The substantive nature of the cultural heritage is dismissed in the schools of the open, pluralistic society. The cultural heritage is no longer viewed as fixed or enduring, and the so-called "subject matters" are seen rather as processive inquiries. For example, history is not the record of past events to be memorized and cherished for its own sake. It is the critical inquiry into the meaning of past events in relation to current and possible future situations. Thus, it is not a body of substantive facts to be imposed upon the mind, but rather a method of evaluating the present and redirecting the future. Similarly, mathematics is a method of reasoning and solving genuine human problems, not an infinite set of irrelevant formulae and equations; language is a method of communication, rather than a set of rules for correct speech and writing; and science is a method of establishing facts and revising axiomatic principles for self-correction, not a mere set of fixed laws.

Briefly, in pluralistic society what the schools transmit are processes of inquiry and methods of dealing with factual situations, not primarily substantive bodies of knowledge. And through these processes and methods the pluralistic society is capable of directing the social reconstruction made possible by its continuing flexibility.

From this perspective, it is not difficult to understand why those educators who are committed primarily to teaching independent subject-matter bodies of truth have accused those who emphasize

Educational values vary as greatly between societies as do the societies themselves.

In a primitive society, education is concerned with teaching the craft by which the family earns a living. These children are learning rug making in Afghanistan.

In a rural society like this community in Peru, an attempt is made to educate the young to the point of learning the basic skills of reading, writing, and counting.

s a nation becomes more developed
s youth are given the basic skills and
en receive more specialized training
nabling them to participate in the
rowth of the country. This secre-
rial class in Gabon will go on to
ll jobs in government and business
fices.

Some educational systems are
used to perpetuate national
ideologies. The scarves worn
by these schoolboys in Uzbek
are symbols of their membership in Young Pioneers, a
group which teaches alle-
giance to Marxism.

Other educational systems teach physical defense for protection of beliefs.
These Peking students are training for the militia.

process and method of being anti-intellectual. For the former, the role of human intelligence is basically passive and receptive. The use of the mind is to know and appreciate the intricate and logical consistencies of facts and laws that rise above the power of human change. Truth endures, and only the mind that endures this truth also endures.

But in the flexible, pluralistic society it is the task of the schools to encourage the development of the kind of intelligence that will refuse merely to accept the existing facts but will, rather, devise practical measures of dealing with these facts, thereby creating new facts that will speak less harshly to human needs and desires.

The Intellectual Foundations of Democratic Pluralism

What are our chances of continuing to improve the democratic qualities of the open, pluralistic society? Whatever they are depends substantially on the concepts underlying our American educational system. Fundamental to the theoretical bases of democratic education is the notion that cultural values are our selective responses to our own sociophysical environments. We are not fixed beings with prescribed, unchangeable natures and predefined purposes, but evolving beings capable of directing the course of our own evolutionary development. Reality is open to both chance and change which afford us the opportunity to improve the conditions of existence. With these philosophical foundations, education does not merely polish what is "given"; it provides the social experiences through which we may, without fixed limitations, constantly and indefinitely perfect our intellectual capacities to identify and resolve social problems and value conflicts.

But the acceptance of these concepts means we must reject the beliefs about human values and experience which have been fervently held since the time when we could envision no practical means of evaluating and revising our social goals or influencing our own futures. Charles Frankel, in *The Case for Modern Man*,[6] has identified and criticized the most formidable concepts by which the belief in intellectual progress as the key to the progress

---

[6] (Boston: Beacon Press, 1959).

of civilization is denied. One such idea, advocated by Jacques Maritain, is centered in the belief that human societies depend on submission to the authority of absolute and eternal values. Frankel argues that social values are not predetermined, but are constructs of experience and subject to empirical evaluation. Therefore, we need not agree on final values in order to live together cooperatively, for social integration is a question of finding ways of resolving value conflicts.

The second concept is that of original sin. According to Reinhold Niebuhr, this concept disallows practical human effort as a means of resolving human problems. Frankel counters with the liberal notion of human perfectibility, by which he means not that there are no limits to human progress, but that whatever limits there are are not necessarily fixed, and that there is no real reason why we should conclude that any problem is beyond our solution.

The third concept, supported by Karl Mannheim, is the denial of the validity of the experimental approach to values on the basis of a denial of man's ability to approach human problems objectively. In other words, the rational, objective methods of science are not applicable to social reform and value reorganization. But Frankel clarifies the meaning of scientific objectivity by showing that man's study of his physical environment need not differ essentially from his study of his social environment. Objectivity is not a psychological attitude, he says, nor is it inevitable that we will always have a biased perspective of human experience and social conditions, for objectivity is the result of cooperative inquiry conducted according to rigorous public rules. Physical scientists isolate and define problems, set criteria of relevance for the gathering of pertinent data, follow established procedures in the construction of hypotheses to be tested, evaluate actions according to their consequences, and hold their tentative conclusions open to public scrutiny. For the objective mind there is no private knowledge, no mysterious source of truth, no facts that are beyond question, no ideas too sacred to be tested by the rigorous criterion of workability, and no established institution, authority, or social operation which is not subject to constant re-evaluation.

There is no reason, Frankel says, why this methodology or some extension or improvement of the scientific method cannot be employed in resolving value conflicts and testing value judgments in light of the consequences of experience.

But Arnold Toynbee has rejected this possibility on the grounds that human history is inexorably patterned by fixed laws which predetermine the course of human societies apart from the efforts of men to direct their own destinies. The experimental liberal argues for the openness of history and the freedom of men, at least in some limited form, which grant the possibility to men of liberating themselves from conditions previously considered inevitable. Thus, Frankel concludes,

> the revolution of modernity has not been only a material revolution or an intellectual revolution. It has been a moral revolution of extraordinary scope, a radical alteration in what the human imagination is prepared to envisage and demand. And it has changed the basic dimensions in which we measure happiness and unhappiness, success and failure. It has given us the sense that we make our own history; it has led us to impose new and more exacting demands on ourselves and our leaders; it has set loose the restless vision of a world in which men might be liberated from age-old burdens, and come to set their own standards and govern their own lives.[7]

The revolution of modernity points out the challenges and the opportunities of democratic education in the pluralistic societies of the future. The school can no longer discharge its responsibilities to society by merely transmitting information and inculcating traditional values. Nor can it do more than this on the assumption that the significant issues of human destiny are resolved by automatic processes operating independently of conscious human effort.

Curriculums comprised of answers to questions of fact and value will not satisfy those who are either disturbed by the disintegration of social norms or stirred by the increasing prospects of directing the course of human history and reordering the conditions of human society. *The relevance of education is its capacity to help students learn how to influence their own futures instead of resigning themselves to supposed inevitabilities.* To meet this test of relevancy, the schools must teach the methods (and provide the confidence) to appraise intelligently the claims of those who shout "Impossible, it cannot be done!"

---

[7] *Ibid.,* pp. 208–209.

Our history abounds with such claims: "Men will not work unless faced by the prospects of starvation"; "Some are born to rule, others to follow"; "Suffering is necessary for human growth and development"; "Learning is an arduous task, not meant to be enjoyed"; "The prosperity of a few requires the poverty of many." Each of these claims, as well as others that are being made today as they have for centuries, are attempts to protect values from the practical test of social consequences. Relevant education will free us not only from false necessities but also from narrow interests. The active role of teaching youth how to resolve value controversies and how to revise conflicting values is the compelling challenge of education that is relevant to both the present and the future.

SUGGESTIONS FOR FURTHER READING

Bronowski, Jacob. *Science and Human Values*. New York: Harper & Row, 1956.

Carr, Edward Hallett. *The New Society*. Boston: Beacon Press, 1966 (9th printing).

Dewey, John. *Theory of Valuation*. Chicago: The University of Chicago Press, 1939.

Frankel, Charles. *The Democratic Prospect*. New York: Harper & Row, 1962.

Gardner, John W. *Self-Renewal, The Individual and the Innovative Society*. New York: Harper & Row, 1963.

Stanley, William O. *Education and Social Integration*. New York: Teachers College, Columbia University, 1953.

PART THREE

The School in American Society

If the rising generation does not grow up with
democratic principles, the fault will lie in
the system of popular education. An ignorant
people can *be* governed, but only a wise
people can *govern itself*.

W. T. HARRIS

"The beginning of wisdom is wonder."
Socrates

Chapter Eight

THE SCHOOL
CURRICULUM

The social purpose of the schools is to teach the young the knowledge, attitudes, skills, and appreciations necessary to become productively participating members of our society. This means teaching both "democratic citizenship" and the necessary know-how for specialization in the many roles which make up our complex society.

Our society, however, which places great emphasis on the dignity and worth of the individual, also expects the schools to educate for individualism. Thus, the history of educational ideology in America has been characterized by conflict and discussion between proponents of both the societal- and individual-oriented aims for education, as well as by many attempts to integrate these goals into a coherent plan for schooling.

The plans for schooling are embodied in statements of the curriculum and school organization procedures. Thus, these plans present "a course to be run" (curriculum) and the procedural ways (school organization) of running it. More specifically, the curriculum is often referred to as the subjects which are taught and the scope and sequencing of these subjects over the school years; and school organization is discussed in terms of three specific levels, elementary (kindergarten through Grade 6), junior high school (Grades 7–9); and senior high school (Grades 10–12). The matter is, of course, much more complicated than this.

The Basic Referents for Schooling

The development of the curriculum and school organization plans is an example of social planning. It is, in fact, one of the few areas in American life in which our society openly supports the concept of public social planning. Large corporations, of course, are engaged in long-range social planning which dramatically affects the lives of all of us, but this kind of planning considered to be in the private sector.

Planning for curriculum and school organization entails the use of three major sources of philosophical and empirical data. These sources, which are often referred to as the "basic referents for schooling," are (1) the nature and needs of our society, (2) the nature and needs of learners, and (3) the nature of knowledge and the relationship between knowledge and social needs. Thus, schools are concerned about whether they serve society adequately, whether they serve the individual in society, and whether they pass on our cultural heritage in an adequate manner.

The school serves society by maintaining the necessary role players to help the society function in its present state. We know, for example, that we will need doctors, lawyers, scientists, engineers, teachers, professors, and skilled workers for a wide variety of jobs. We know, further, that all citizens will be called upon to vote and to exercise critical judgment in their participation in the affairs of their communities.

The school serves the learner when it provides opportunity for the development of individual potentiality. We know that each person is biologically unique, that each person must live in the human condition of mortality, and that each person must find meaning and fulfillment in his existence through self-development.

Our cultural heritage is the past's contribution to mankind. It is our most precious human heritage in that it represents hard-won knowledge, ideas, skills, appreciations, and attitudes which have raised man from a primitive state to his present level of development. Throughout the course of this development our knowledge has become specialized in the form of academic disciplines with their special ways of thinking and discovering, and it is these disciplines which form the third referent for schooling.

THE PROBLEM OF PRIORITY

Granted that there can be no real schooling in which individual learners do not learn, that schools cannot exist without performing a service to society, and that there is nothing to teach which is not some form of subject matter, there is still the matter of priorities to consider. Which referent is the core value of schooling?

In many ways it is a matter of beginnings. If we begin with one referent and then proceed to raise questions about its relevance to the other two, we tend to come up with different kinds of plans than if we had begun with either of the other referents. For example, if we begin with subject matter, concern for the individual tends to become a technical problem of how to manage the learning situation so that individuals may master the cultural heritage in a logically sequenced manner. On the other hand, if the individual is the beginning point, subject matter tends to be seen as a body of knowledge, attitudes, and skills which can be related to the needs, interests, and activities of the individual as he develops his own unique personality and potentiality in the context of the schools.

In essence, schools cannot serve three masters at one time, and traditionally the disciplines of knowledge or subject matters have been the central concern of the schools. In the past, considerable friction existed between the school and society because of this orientation. Formal education was considered "impractical" in comparison to the "school of hard knocks," which was more highly valued. Today, there is much less of a gap between the subject-matter-oriented schools and society because our society has become a highly complex technological system which is now directly dependent upon specialists and the knowledge and skills they learn in the schools.

Now that subject matter and societal aims are more unified,

the crucial question relates to the effect of subject matter and society upon the individual. The chief concern at present is about such modern phenomena as the depersonalization and alienation of human beings in contemporary life; the bureaucratization of social relationships; the possibility of men becoming slaves to the "things" created by their technological sophistication; and the reality of "thought control," "brainwashing," and other social engineering practices. The central question really is, What effect does the dominant curriculum and school organization have upon the development of individual potentiality?

THE INADEQUACY OF THE PRESENT CURRICULUM

We can be rather certain that the present curriculum is not adequate for large numbers of our youth. For example, the so-called culturally deprived youth often found in cities (but also in certain non-urban regions such as Appalachia) are quite obviously not succeeding in developing their potentialities in today's schools. The dropout rate is relatively high for these youth and the comparative scores on standardized tests show large average differences between certain groups of culturally deprived students and their more fortunate peers.

Recent studies[1] initiated by the United States Office of Education, involving six hundred thousand children in about four thousand schools indicate serious problems. Among the findings of these studies are the following: (1) minority groups are segregated (65 per cent of Negroes go to schools in which more than 90 per cent of the students are Negroes); (2) educational facilities are poorer in the South and the non-metropolitan North; (3) there are substantial average score differences between racial and ethnic groups in a variety of tests and at all grade levels; and (4) different educational opportunities have a greater effect on general ability measures (I.Q., for example) than upon measures of achievement; the latter are more closely related to socioeconomic level than with measures of school program quality.

Further evidence of the inadequacy of the present curriculum

[1] James Coleman *et al., Equality of Educational Opportunity,* Office of Education, Department of Health, Education and Welfare (Washington: Government Printing Office, 1966).

"For example the so-called culturally deprived youth often found in cities are quite obviously not succeeding in developing their potentialities in today's schools."

and/or forms of schooling can be found in Benjamin Bloom's *Stability and Change in Human Characteristics.*[2] Bloom's work presents rather dramatic evidence that school achievement potential is set very early and that it becomes predictable for groups of youngsters sometime during the middle grade period (Grades 3 to 6, among children eight to eleven years old).

Although many schools are presently immersed in considerable innovative activity in an attempt to reach "deprived" youngsters, there is as yet no hard evidence that these attempts will be successful. The early results reported for "Operation Headstart" (the government-sponsored pre-school program for deprived youngsters) suggest that any noticeable changes that occur during the program are soon washed out in the regular school situation.

[2] (New York: John Wiley & Sons, 1964).

At present, the conclusion can only be what we have known all along — that public school curricula are constructed primarily for the college-bound student and that the subject matter studied has relatively little direct relevance to youngsters' lives in any immediate sense.

Success in such a program demands a strong motivation for success and a superiority in a restricted number of potential abilities and/or talents. If one wished all children who attend school to have the greatest chance for success in school it would be wise to send only the children of professionals in a high income bracket who are white Anglo-Saxon Protestants (or Jewish), living in the metropolitan North. (And by all means send them to an Ivy League college). On the other hand, we could do away with the present curriculum (indeed, it would collapse) if we sent only children of unskilled, poverty-stricken, Negro, southern rural parents to school. The steps and combinations of income, class, and ethnic and racial differences fall into a fairly identifiable pattern between these two extremes.

In substance, then, the curriculum cannot be taken for granted unless we wish to uphold a position which is already untenable for many American children. And, if we were to do something to remedy the current situation, where would we begin?

Five Determiners of the Curriculum

There are five general ideas regarding the direction schooling should take. They are not mutually exclusive in the sense that they do not involve each other in their implications, but they do identify five pivotal points for getting some leverage on the problems which plague the schools.

1. THE CURRICULUM AS DETERMINED BY THE DISCIPLINES OF KNOWLEDGE

Many persons argue that the curriculum, if it is to have any cultural meaning, must be soundly based in the disciplines of knowledge and that, furthermore, improvement in the development of the curriculum lies in the meaningful presentation of subject matter to pupils.

Above, in a Head Start program, pre-school children receive health care, individual attention and an opportunity to work together. Below, Job Corps members are at work on a conservation project. These high school dropouts are taught useful skills while receiving education in a less rigid environment.

Many present-day efforts are illustrative of this position. Considerable effort is being spent today to identify the "structure" of each discipline (i.e., mathematics, the sciences, etc.). The structure refers to some general framework of key ideas or generalizations that are basic to each subject. Once having found this structure, we can proceed to present it to youngsters in the most logical way, tailored to the cognitive abilities of children at each level.

Concomitantly, emphasis is being placed upon the discovery of knowledge by use of the mode (or modes) of inquiry characteristic of each discipline (e.g., the methods of science). Facts alone are isolated and unless they are related to a general structure they will be meaningless and soon forgotten. Also, the doubling of human knowledge every eight to ten years makes the mastery of all facts an absolute impossibility (if it ever was possible after about 1600). Therefore, the important thing is to be able to understand and utilize the processes of discovering and/or creating knowledge in the disciplines.

The curriculum, then, ought to be organized around these basic structures of the disciplines and modes of inquiry so that it will be an integrated, coherent pattern of logical experiences over the years. This, it is argued, would provide a reorganization of knowledge in the schools which would update the present content and provide a meaningful order which could be understood by all (or most) youngsters and increase the cumulative impact of the curriculum on learning.

Most schoolmen are agreed that the reorganization and updating of the content or subject matter is a very needed and positive step toward improving the curriculum. There is no quarrel with the idea that the schools would not be schools without the knowledge to be gained there. The problem arises when one considers whether this is enough to improve schooling, or whether this is even the crucial area, (as useful as such plans for reorganization and updating it purport to be).

2. THE CURRICULUM AS TEACHER-DETERMINED

After all, it can be argued, when the teacher shuts the door and begins to teach, even the best curricular decision is only as good as the teacher's knowledge, skill, and ability to put it into action.

Teachers who do not know their subject matter, or who are

The Teachers' Corps is a program designed to attract qualified college graduates who have not fulfilled specific certification requirements. These potential teachers train in the classroom while also attending classes related to their training.

personally unsuited for teaching, or who lack the ability to translate knowledge and ideas into productive student activities, cannot hope to make the best out of *any* form of subject matter. It is more imperative, it is argued, to emphasize the selection and training of teachers rather than the reorganization of subject matter.

Teacher training institutions and teacher education programs in colleges and universities have come under heavy attack during the past ten years, notably in two studies, one by Conant[3] and the other by Koerner.[4] These studies have concluded generally that there is too much red tape and bureaucratic control involved in the training and certification of teachers; that there is too much

[3] James Bryant Conant, *The Education of American Teachers* (New York: McGraw-Hill Book Co., 1963).
[4] James Koerner, *The Miseducation of American Teachers* (Boston: Houghton Mifflin Company, 1963).

professional education and not enough "solid content" in the programs; and that the teacher education portion of the program is often repetitive and full of trivial generalizations of little value. It has also been noted that there is a great lack of any definitive evidence connecting teacher education programs and later teacher performance and/or students' learning in schools (on the job).

The objections to teacher-determined curricula come from many quarters and for many reasons. For years we have known that education students as a group, those training to be teachers, do not usually come from the upper level of achievement ranges among college students. Furthermore, there have been questions raised concerning personality factors in the selection of teachers; in the opinion of these critics, security-oriented and timid types of persons are favored by the schools. Salary factors have also been noted. Teachers' salaries are low in comparison to those of persons of similar commitment to training (excepting perhaps nurses and social workers), and in a society in which success seems to be embedded in material values, it has been argued that only the potentially unsuccessful will teach.

A further compounding fact is the social mobility of teachers. Teachers frequently (all out of proportion to numbers) come from lower middle class families for which becoming a teacher provides mobility up the social ladder. Or, for those of higher classes, who might lose status if forced to enter other occupations, it becomes a step to sliding down the ladder.

The teaching wife also raises questions. Many teachers are married women who are contributing a second salary to their families. They are usually tied to their husbands' jobs (in terms of residence), and because of family responsibilities, are perhaps more loath to make a full professional commitment to program development or full professional growth. It is, however, less certain what effect this factor has on personnel than some of those mentioned above.

Studies of teachers show that there is a heavy turnover in teaching. A ten-year study of one thousand University of Illinois[5] graduates suggests some startling problems. In this study it was found

[5] W. W. Charters, Jr., "Survival in the Profession: A Criterion for Selecting Teacher Trainees," *Journal of Teacher Education,* 7 (September, 1956), pp. 253–255.

that 40 per cent of the teachers in training never taught after graduation. Furthermore, one-half of the remaining 60 per cent had dropped out of teaching at the end of the second year. After five years there were only 150 of the original one thousand in teaching, and less than one hundred were left at the end of the tenth year.

Teachers are also highly mobile. Women teachers tend to move in and out of the profession, and men teachers tend to move up (to administrative jobs) or out.

At the elementary level about 85 per cent are women, and 50 per cent of high school teachers are women. The profession thus takes on some of the general social characteristics of women's occupations — e.g., high turnover, discontinuity in careers, flight of men, and lack of occupational solidity. In the circumstances, it is often all a superintendent can do to get enough "bodies" in the classroom, to say nothing of qualified professional persons.

It does seem that attention to the selection and training of teachers can be a promising avenue of improvement. Nevertheless, teachers work in a school system and are in many ways affected by the policies, plans, and working conditions found there; furthermore, the teaching profession does not show the stability of most professional groups and this raises questions about the qualifications of teachers to determine the curriculum.

3. THE CURRICULUM AS DETERMINED BY THE LEARNERS

Objections may be raised to both teacher- and subject-matter-determined programs. It is, after all, the student who must do the learning.

Perhaps the most unchallenged knowledge we possess that is relevant to schooling is the fact of individual differences. Each student comes to school as a biologically and psychologically unique organism. Furthermore, we know that learning is related not only to capacity but also to the values, aspirations, perceptions, needs, and interests of individual learners. Thus, it is almost impossible for any two individuals to be equally ready to learn the same things in the same manner at the same time in all or even many aspects of the curriculum.

This being the case, it has often been argued over the years that the curriculum should be determined by the learner as he relates to knowledge and to the social conditions of the school and society he lives in.

This means, in effect, that the school should provide the most stimulating and culturally significant environment it can for children, while the teacher, rather than taking the learners through a prefocused sequence, acts as guide, helper, and resource person. In this role the teacher attempts to develop the learners' awareness of the potential significance of the school environment and the alternatives available to them, and to facilitate by his presence and maturity the planning, developing, and experiencing of meaningful activities.

Two major objections have been raised concerning this approach, one on the ground of practicality and the other on the basis of the proper function of the school in society.

Many teachers are convinced of the desirability of a student-centered curriculum. In most cases, however, this type of curriculum is viewed as an ideal rather than a practical plan of action. By and large, teachers either are not, or do not feel, capable of individualizing programs and playing the necessary roles involved in this approach to teaching.

To begin with, previous school experiences have not provided models for teachers to imitate. Consequently, teachers have little "feel" for implementing a student-centered approach. Furthermore, although the rationale is appealing and even convincing, the techniques and methods for implementing such an approach are difficult to identify. Thus teachers are called upon, it is argued, to perform in a flexible, creative way that few are capable of or secure enough to try. It has often been said that a student-centered curriculum would be practical only if all teachers were excellent. Therefore, it is said to be desirable but impractical.

But many persons do not even admit the desirability of a student-centered curriculum, maintaining that it is not only highly unrealistic but "soft-minded" or "sentimental" as well. They argue that schools are preparation for life and that a student-centered situation is a highly unrealistic picture of reality, that society will make demands upon students to be competent in specific ways and to enter into the general competitive life, and that the student-centered curriculum cannot assure readiness for either of these exigencies.

The scholar adds further objections. The schools, he argues, exist to pass on the cultural heritage and to prepare future generations to further the creation of new knowledge. Both of these tasks demand a systematic and thorough background in the disciplines of knowledge. The best, and perhaps only way to do this, it is proposed, is to organize this knowledge in a rational manner and systematically teach it to the young. A student-centered approach cannot do this; in fact it would defeat the basic purpose of the schools.

4. The Curriculum as Determined by the School System

Many people are coming to think that the organizational structure of the schools may be more relevant than either the persons involved (teachers and students) or the subject matter.

Each school district in America has its own school board, central administration(s), school organizational plan, school building administrator, public relation policies, and curricular plans. This organization, and the personnel involved, form a complex set of interacting forces which create a sociopsychological climate of impressive force that affects each teacher and learner.

Social psychologists argue that the best way to effect improvement in any organizational endeavor is to change the system itself, rather than to tinker with specific parts of it.[6] Thus, in school terms, basic system changes might be brought about by removing local control of school boards and instituting some kind of regional or national control, by changing the authority and status system, or by some other major realignment.

What is needed, according to this position, is a change basic enough to force persons in the system to behave differently from the way they did before (and, it is hoped, in a more productive way). This position has some fairly sound evidence to support it. We are affected by the norms of the persons we work and interact with, and we do often change when conditions are such that we can no longer do the same things and get the same results. Studies of innovations such as team teaching and ungraded

[6] Daniel Katz and Robert Kahn, *The Social-Psychology of Organizations* (New York: John Wiley & Sons, 1966).

and/or multi-age grouping suggest that teachers do develop different ways of coping with teaching when placed in new situations. Imagine, for example, a teacher taken from a grade level classroom (say grade 4) having twenty-five students and put in charge of a multi-aged group of one hundred heterogeneous fourth, fifth, and sixth graders, along with three other teachers. It would simply be impossible for this teacher to proceed in her former manner, with children of age differences of four to five years and achievement differences ranging anywhere from two to twelve years in specific areas, to say nothing of having to plan and teach with three other teachers as well.

This approach has certain obvious merits. Yet it can be argued that in essence it tends to result in change for change's sake, and not change which is focused upon the development of specific school goals. Therefore, changing the organizational focus and processes in the school does not necessarily insure that students will be more meaningfully involved in their work, nor does it insure that teachers will be more competently employed, or that the disciplines of knowledge will be more adequately presented. In addition, organizational manipulation raises certain ethical problems concerning the changing of staff and student behavior without benefit of rational choice on the part of staff and students.

5. THE CURRICULUM AS SOCIETALLY DETERMINED

At the broadest level, there are some who adhere to the social system determination of the curriculum. Regardless of school system variations, teacher personnel, or content, it is argued that the ability, motivation, and personal response to curriculum is so definitely set in the learner by his social situation that the only way to improve schooling is through broad and sweeping social reform.

The problem of many Negroes in contemporary American life is a case in point. By and large, the Negro child comes to school from an uneducated family of low income. He has had few of the advantages of toys, parental stimulation in language experiences, travel, or parental models of educated persons.

Further, he has felt prejudice and is already a part of what Michael Harrington calls "the culture of poverty,"[7] which means

[7] Michael Harrington, *The Other America* (Baltimore: Penguin Books, 1964).

he has internalized the hopelessness and helplessness of his culture. He has little if any aspiration to succeed.

To help future Negro children, it is argued, we must break down the segregation and poverty barriers as well as increase educational opportunity, for a vicious cycle exists today. A better job means more money. More money means better living conditions (providing the Negro can escape the "ghetto"). Better living conditions means more motivation for learning in children and thus an increased chance for school success. Success truly breeds success; the "catch" is that few Negroes have the educational background to get better jobs. And so, like a cat chasing his tail, one goes from education to job to housing, and back to education in a vain attempt to better the Negro's chances for success. The least likely place to break this cycle, according to this position, is in education. At the very least, a concerted effort on all fronts would be needed.

The Negro serves only as a dramatic example here. If we analyzed other groups and individuals from this viewpoint, we might well see that the general conditions of their social life fairly well predetermines the value of their school experiences to them (and to society). The recent concern for the gifted student has a similar rationale. Although we are often more prone to think of the gifted as genetically superior and the academically retarded as socially deprived, one can argue that many of the gifted are beneficiaries of excellent social circumstances and that socioeconomic background may be at least a partial reason for their superior performance on I.Q. tests and other school tasks. This may or may not be true of those individuals classified as geniuses, but it does seem to be true of those having I.Q.'s of 125–145.

If we magnify the social determinist position by changing our focus from the individual or group of learners to the needs of society as a whole, we are faced with further curricular implications.

Our nation is engaged in a world power struggle. Furthermore, we are a highly organized society economically. Because of both of these factors, we need large numbers of trained persons to fulfill our national and international obligations. In these circumstances it is highly doubtful that our society would condone a curriculum that did not meet these needs, no matter what the cost to given individuals or minority groups. The curriculum, then, might be said to be plagued by various pressures to produce the needed role players for our society.

Dropouts are natural consequences of such pressures. They are, in a sense, proof that the system is working. Since the skills to run a highly technological system are, for the most part, abstract, take a long time to develop, and require a limited set (potentially) of human abilities, the schools must "waste" many to get the few (relative to the many) that are needed.

This has been the pattern of the development of our "natural" resources in America. Growth has always been accompanied by tremendous waste of material. Thus, it would not be surprising that human resources would be wasted in the wake of the pressure of social needs. According to this view, the curriculum then, no matter what the scholars, or teachers, or administrators, or learners say, will in the long run reflect the pressures of the various needs of the social system.

Recent Curricular Development

CURRICULAR DEVELOPMENT IN THE DISCIPLINES

The great activity in the area of curricular development during the past ten years[8] has taken a common course. By and large, concern for national needs, especially the need for scientists, engineers, and mathematicians, has caused persons outside professional education to push for curricular change. This interest has been followed by large grants of federal and private foundation funds to bring scholars together to revise curricula. These revisions are then submitted to (or developed in conjunction with) selected public school teachers and pilot-tested in a small number of schools. After a second or third revision the new programs are released for general school use.

A number of key points are worth noting with reference to the previous discussion about curricular determinants. First, these programs are usually instigated by pressures and persons not directly connected with the schools. Second, they are usually subject-matter oriented. Third, they rarely involve specific local

[8] Robert W. Heath, *New Curricula* (New York: Harper & Row, 1964).

Knowledge gained from psychological research should be applied to curriculum development. This Harvard School of Education professor is studying the spontaneous language development of children of different ages, social backgrounds and ethnic groups. One child verbalizes a situation while the other points to the appropriate picture.

school system participation; and finally, they involve teachers only minimally (although extensive in-service programs often follow after the change has been made).

Federal Programs: Title III

In 1965, Congress passed the Elementary and Secondary Education Act. Under Title III of this Act, a portion of the funds provided were set aside for "innovation and dissemination." Local school districts may apply to the U.S. Office of Education for funds for the establishment of new programs. If the application is accepted, then the local school district is given money to "innovate" and to "disseminate" their new practices.

It should be noted that these funds are provided by Congress (an outside agency responding to national pressures and concerns), but they go directly to school systems and involve some

193

participation by teachers. Thus, the school system is a key element in curricular development under the provisions of Title III.

THE WISCONSIN IMPROVEMENT PROGRAM

Under this program, sponsored by the Ford Foundation, more than a million dollars have been given to the University of Wisconsin during the past ten years to foster the development of team teaching in the state. Professional educators from the University of Wisconsin, in conjunction with local school districts, have developed team teaching programs throughout the state. The student teaching of University and state college students has often been integrated with these teams. Thus, this project has focused upon teachers, in both inservice and preservice capacities.

Here, also, it may be noted that outside agencies have funded improvement in response to national concerns. The focus upon teachers and organization reflects the idea that the teacher and the school system are the crucial elements in curricular determination.

INDUSTRY AND EDUCATION

The textbook industry has been involved in curriculum making for many years. Many private companies have produced textbooks, which, in all too many cases, have been slavishly followed by teachers. This in effect has meant that the curriculum has been developed by authors paid by industry to write books that will sell to schools at a profit for the company.

As a part of contemporary mass media, textbooks are perhaps a positive force. Yet many such products are geared to the "lowest common denominator" that will produce the highest profit. Television programming is an excellent example of this process. Textbooks have not completely escaped the problems of other mass media, however. Often, rather than attempting to upgrade content, the authors, editors, and publishers have considered only consumer appeal in the materials they present in their books. This has meant that new material is not presented very often, since it would require relearning on the part of teachers (the consumers). Until the past few years, at least, it has also meant that textbooks have steered clear of portraying some of the vital concerns of our society, such as the status of minority groups, sex in American life, and foreign governmental systems. Regional differences have also affected the textbook publishing industry; material that may offend teachers living in certain regions of the country may be cut and more appealing material substituted.

With the advent of teaching machines and automation industry has greatly expanded its participation in curricular development. Although exact figures are impossible to compute, it is estimated that many millions of dollars are being spent by industries to develop new products for sale to the schools. The market is a huge one, for it has been estimated by the U. S. Office of Education that some 48.8 billion dollars would be spent by colleges and schools during the 1967 fiscal year. Of this, it was expected that most would go for salaries, buildings, maintenance, and textbooks, but that at least one billion dollars would go into aids such as slide and movie projectors, tape recorders, closed circuit TV, and teaching machines. The federal government is currently funding a number of industries for the development of automated instructional systems and computerized programming. If the previous pattern holds, once the industries have completed the construction of these devices they will be allowed to sell them to the schools for profit.

Industrial interest in the educational market can be seen in the growth of mergers in recent years. It is estimated that during the past two years at least 120 mergers and combines have been set up to exploit the education market. For example, General Electric and Time, Inc. have formed a joint venture called General Learning Corporation, which includes the Silver Burdett textbook publishing subsidiary of Time, Inc.

These mergers and outlays of money mean that industry has stepped up its role in schooling. We may well see the textbook replaced in favor of a complete automated instructional system in years to come. The effect of this change on the curriculum would, of course, be phenomenal. We may even move into an era in which school systems and teachers are only minimally involved in the instruction of students. This is still in the future, of course, but the trend toward the development of curricula by industry for profit creates many problems.

In essence, then, the special programs and trends described above illustrate the involvement of all key determinants of the curriculum (except the student), although emphasis is placed on one or more different determinants in each specific case. The plain truth of the matter is that no one is quite sure how best to develop curricula, and the fact that few curricular changes took place prior to the expenditure of large federal and foundation funds during the past ten years may be evidence of this.

The Organization of the School System

It is obvious from the previous discussion that the broad social, economic, and political climate and activity in our nation, states, and communities affect school curricula in many ways. Yet, at the level of actual learning, we must look primarily at the school system itself to understand the curriculum.

THE SYSTEMS METAPHOR

The school system is an organization which, like most contemporary organizations, tends to be bureaucratic in structure. It encompasses status and roles, a hierarchy of authority, and numerous policies which are developed to facilitate operational efficiency. Definite boundaries (geographical locations, facilities, jobs, etc.) distinguish the school from other social institutions, however, and within these boundaries a system of working relationships has been developed.

The concept of systems is quite prominent in social science literature today. Taken from the physical and biological sciences, it is utilized to explain organizational life in social institutions, the major difference being that the key units of analysis are, for example, no longer atoms or molecules, or red and white corpuscles, but human events that are structured and reasonably predictable. Thus, in a department store or school one can specify the events (i.e., selling, teaching, etc.) that must take place to make the system work. Furthermore, the policies, authority, communication and facilities can be specified in relation to these events, and such specification produces organizational expectancies and norms which tend to make the events predictable.

The systems metaphor may be used to explain the nature of the curriculum in the schools. The balance of this section will deal with this phenomenon.

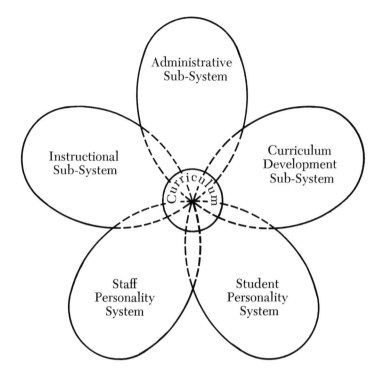

FIGURE 3

The School System

FIVE SUB-SYSTEMS

The school system may be divided into five sub-systems, as shown in Figure 3, which are analytically discrete. The managerial or administrative sub-system acts both as a major contact with the outer world and as a manager of the inner system; the curriculum development sub-system is charged with the production of plans for subject matter and school organization to facilitate the goals of the system; and the instructional sub-systems usually classrooms, include the teaching-learning situations and interactions beyond the curriculum plans or administration.

If we limit the administrative system to managerial activities such as grading, testing, record keeping, making regulations, and supervising; the curriculum development system to in-service meetings on some subject such as mathematics; and the instructional system to a single classroom where the teaching of this subject is carried on, we begin to see the complex interaction of these three systems in the school. Add to this the different teacher personality systems and their effect upon all three social systems in terms of abilities, knowledge, attitudes, and skills, plus the individual student's abilities, past experience, attitudes, and aspirations, and we begin to understand something of the complexity of the curriculum.

The curriculum evolves out of the interaction of these subsystems in the schools, as shown in Figure 3. For example, let us take Student A, a boy with an I.Q. of 100 from a lower class family. He will perceive mathematics in terms of his own background of success and cultural aspirations. Now let us place Student A with Teacher X, who is a forty-year-old mother of two, returning to teaching after many years at home. Teacher X has her own personality and her own knowledge of mathematics. Furthermore, her interest and vitality and her concept of teaching and its rewards will be unique to her.

But there are other students in the classroom, and both X and A will be affected by their personalities. Student A may not work hard because that would be a violation of peer group standards. Teacher X may not exert much effort in teaching because the class is full of lower class youngsters who are not motivated toward success in school.

Meanwhile, Teacher X may be involved in an in-service education course on modern mathematics in the curriculum development system. She may be trying to learn the new math but finding it highly abstract and too difficult for either her or her students. Yet she will still be expected to teach the new math in her classroom. She may also be forced by administrative regulations to administer tests, grade, and promote in accordance with strict standards or suffer the disapproval of or even dismissal by the administrative staff. And Student A must also perform in accordance with these standards or suffer the consequences of failure.

Out of this complex series of interaction systems some learning will take place for A. What he actually learns will, for his purposes, *be* the curriculum. This learning will have been affected by the administrative policies, the curricular plan, the instructional setting, the personality of his teacher, the norms of his peer group, and his own personality. It is in this way that the curriculum may be said to evolve out of the school system.

The curriculum, then, is a vastly more complicated phenomenon than the plan, course of study, or textbook. It is affected by many forces interacting together in the school system, as well as by agencies outside the school.

Knowledge and the Curriculum

It should be clear from the above discussion that the curriculum is much more than subjects and the information, understandings, skills, attitudes, and appreciations associated with them. Yet our cultural heritage is of central concern in schooling. It is, in the long run, the justification for schooling, whether or not one feels that it is good "just" to "know things" for their own sake, to know them in order to use them for social purposes, or to know them in order to develop one's own potentiality.

Regardless of our purposes in learning, however, an understanding of symbolism is crucial to an understanding of the nature of knowledge. We know that man is a symbol user. Suzanne Langer even suggests that man has a need to transform reality symbolically.[9] Cassirer states it somewhat differently but succinctly when he says that a symbol intervenes between each stimulus and response.[10] Some modern learning theorists talk about this as the organism mediating the environment.

What this means quite simply is that the real world is as much in our heads in the form of symbols (ideas, words, numbers, myths, etc.) as it is "out there" in the form of concrete objects, that man makes his world symbolically out of the raw material of the universe. Therefore, to be human means to possess language and other symbols and to be able to communicate, understand, and share a symbolic system with others.

[9] Suzanne Langer, *Philosophy in a New Key* (New York: The New American Library of World Literature [Mentor Books] 1942).

[10] Ernest Cassirer, *An Essay on Man* (New Haven, Conn.: Yale University Press, 1944).

One comes to realize one's potentiality through understanding our symbolic universe. For example, it is one thing to be able to converse about the world in our common social language but quite another thing to be able to think or converse about it mathematically, or scientifically, or artistically. It even makes a considerable difference to experience the common social world in a foreign language system. Thus, human potentiality is related to coming to "see" the world, or to "be in" the world of man's symbolic systems.

Over the centuries men have built up a series of ways of talking about the world, and/or experiencing the world with symbols. The earliest men used a common language, myths, rituals, simple tools, and artifacts to symbolize and experience living. As the community structure became more complicated, and as technology increased, new symbols were created, and each new discourse opened the way for new methods of experiencing reality. The result of this development may be seen in the wide variety of special disciplines we have today.

Our disciplines of knowledge may be grouped loosely into three categories: the sciences, the humanities, and mathematics. A typical American public high school might classify the disciplines this way: (1) the physical sciences (general science, biology, chemistry, physics) and the social sciences (history, geography, civics, social problems, economics), (2) the humanities (art, music, dance, literature, language), and (3) mathematics (business arithmetic, algebra, geometry, trigonometry, calculus).

Knowing *that* something is such and such a way is not the only kind of knowing, however. Gilbert Ryle, among others, has pointed out that knowing *how* is also important.[11] Thus the school subjects also carry much "know-how." Some of this "know-how" is singled out for the practical courses such as shop, reading, spelling, and physical education, and other "know-how" is built into the more academic courses.

In recent years, with the rapidly increasing growth of knowledge, the so-called academic disciplines have become much more concerned with the "know-how" of their content. This is so quite

---

[11] Gilbert Ryle, *The Concept of Mind* (New York: Barnes and Noble, 1949).

simply because it is becoming increasingly evident that it is humanly impossible for anyone to know all *that* there is to know about all subjects, or even any one subject. Thus, the emphasis has shifted to understanding general ideas in each subject and to learning how to use the methods of inquiry of each field to discover knowledge for oneself. This process has often been called "learning how to learn." Dewey called it "reflective thinking."[12]

The subjects we teach in school are, thus, not arbitrary impositions on students, although it is unfortunately more often true than not that they experience and perceive them in this manner. What is intended, in the best of all possible school worlds, is that the student will come to appreciate the symbolic creations that have been built up through the centuries so that he may live in the most satisfying and self-fulfilling way in relation to others.

We must point out, however, that the academic disciplines, vocational areas, and the derivative subjects we teach in the schools are not the only sources of man's knowledge or perceptual and symbolic experiences. There are many phenomena in life which men (at least some) encounter that are not nearly so easily organized or neatly packaged into sets of related ideas or structures. For example, extra-sensory perception, as experienced through clairvoyance, precognition, premonitions, and dreams, may be said to be a further possible source of knowing. What we often call insight is also not clearly understood as a psychological process, yet no one can deny its importance as a source of problem solving and "know-how."

An allied process, though highly specific in focus, is that of revelation. Many religious leaders over the centuries have claimed that knowledge or truth has been revealed to them by God. Also, mystics and others have reported experiences which do not fall into the usual patterns of knowledge. Visions, experiences of "oneness" or harmony with the universe, a sense of great inner peace, and a knowing "beyond" words are commonly reported mystical or psychological phenomena. Then, too, modern psychological "mystics" have used psychedelic drugs to experience states

[12] John Dewey, *How We Think* (Boston: D. C. Heath & Company, 1933).

of perceptual and symbolic being which are apparently not available to our normal conscious activity, and experiments with hypnosis reveal some startling things about persons that they were not aware of.

These experiences that are beyond the usual concept of knowledge as experienced in the schools (both "knowing how" and "knowing that") cannot be simply discounted. They may, in fact, become much better understood as we continue our historical journey and may in the end lead us to sources of knowing which will be far beyond our present conceptions. Thus, though we should continue to value our present subject matter, we should also realize that not only knowledge grows and changes, but that our concept of knowledge itself undergoes a process of revision and expansion during the process of total human development.

The Future of the Curriculum

This is an exciting time in the field of education. So much is happening today that it is almost impossible to see clearly what the shape of schools will become. Nevertheless, there are signs that indicate some possible directions.

On the International Scene. As long as the cold war continues there will be serious and pressing demands made upon the schools for personnel to maintain our national security.

On the National Scene. With the advent of tremendously increased federal spending (8.6 billion dollars in fiscal year 1967 as against 2.3 billion in fiscal year 1964) the schools will be forced to innovate and to modify current procedures in many ways. Some increased federal direction (even if only incidental) will be sure to follow.

Furthermore, the entrance of industry into education en masse will mean a lessening of local and professional control of curricula; it is also possible that private industry will play the federal role.

A national testing move is afoot. Its first phase will begin soon and this could well mean the slow put steady standardization of curricula throughout the country.

In the Study of Human Nature. Exciting new findings concerning the human potential to learn, perceive, know, and experience are beginning to emerge. The implications of these findings are still far from clear in terms of schooling. Still, some of the psychological, sociological, anthropological, and philosophical trends offer hope for a much better understanding of human nature than we have at present.

In the Schools. The advent of automation and technology in the schools may drastically change the present teaching–learning situation and/or the teacher's job.

The development of drugs which may increase memory or expand consciousness may have some impact on schooling.

As autotelic environments become more and more prominent, we may see a lessening of emphasis upon such traditional areas as reading and handwriting. Learning may be facilitated by head phones during sleep, increased listening speeds, and other audiovisual techniques.

In spite of these new developments, however, the schools are heavily weighted with tradition. Teachers tend to teach the way they were taught, programs tend to remain the same, and outdated content is kept simply because it is well known and understood. Thus, the school system, like many other human institutions, tends to hold onto the familiar; the difficulty of changing old habits is sometimes overwhelming, and parents apparently often feel better when their children are learning what they learned in school.

Altogether, the pressures and trends toward change enumerated above are strong, but so are the old traditions. Therefore, the curriculum of the future is an unknown quantity. One thing we can be certain of, however, is that the next decade or so, at least, will be an exciting, disturbing, and conflict-producing one for all those concerned with the school curriculum.

SUGGESTIONS FOR FURTHER READING

Anderson, Robert M. *Teaching in a World of Change.* New York: Harcourt, Brace & World, 1966.

Bailyn, Bernard. *Education and the Forming of American Society*. Chapel Hill, N.C.: University of North Carolina Press, 1960.

Bode, Boyd H. *Modern Educational Theories*. New York: The Macmillan Co., 1927.

Brim, O. G. *Sociology and the Field of Education*. New York: Russell Sage Foundation, 1958.

Broudy, Harry S., B. Othanel Smith, and Joe R. Burnett. *Democracy and Excellence in American Secondary Schools*. Chicago: Rand McNally & Co., 1964.

"Changing Curriculum Content," prepared by William Alexander. Washington: National Education Association, Association for Supervision and Curriculum Development, 1964.

Cicourel, A. V., and J. I. Kitsuse. *The Educational Decision Makers*. Indianapolis: The Bobbs-Merrill Company, 1963.

Clark, Burton R. *Educating the Expert Society*. San Francisco: Chandler Publishing Co., 1962.

———. "Sociology of Education," in *Handbook of Modern Sociology*, ed. Robert E. Faris. Chicago: Rand McNally & Co., 1964. Pp. 734–769.

Goodlad, John, *et al. The Changing School Curriculum*. New York: The Fund for the Advancement of Education,

Gordon, C. W. *The Social System of the High School*. Glencoe, Ill.: The Free Press, 1957.

Haney, Richard E. "The Changing Curriculum: Science." Washington: National Education Association, Association for Supervision and Curriculum Development, 1967.

Hollingshead, August B. *Elmtown's Youth*. New York: John Wiley & Sons, 1959.

Kimball, Solon T., and James E. McClellan, Jr. *Education and the New America*. New York: Random House, 1962.

King, Arthur R., Jr., and John A. Brownell, *The Curriculum and the Disciplines of Knowledge*. New York: John Wiley & Sons, 1966.

Lieberman, Myron. *Education as a Profession.* Englewood Cliffs, N.J.: Prentice-Hall, 1956.

National Education Association, Association for Supervision and Curriculum Development. "A Climate for Individuality." Washington: The Association, 1965.

———. "What Are the Sources of the Curriculum?" Washington: The Association, 1962.

Stiles, Lindley J. (ed.). *The Teacher's Role in American Society.* New York: Harper & Brothers, 1957.

The results of psychological tests like the one being given here can help to improve both teaching and learning.

Chapter Nine

SCHOOL
SYSTEM ROLES

The school system functions and achieves its purposes by identifying the various roles of persons within the system and by defining role expectations. These roles are assigned within the three social sub-systems discussed in Chapter Eight: the administrative, the curriculum development, and the instructional. They are specialized and interrelated. Furthermore, a person in a school system may play more than one role. This is true, for example, of most teachers, who have a role in both the classroom (instructional sub-system) and the curriculum development sub-system. Figure 4, on page 208, shows the school system and its three major social sub-systems.

Personality systems do not lend themselves easily to role definition, although there may be times when attempts are made to match specific personality traits with special role expectations. By and large, however, such matching is accomplished through the career choices of individuals before they enter the school system.

207

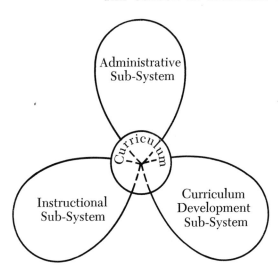

FIGURE 4

Three Social Sub-Systems of the School System

Sub-System Functions and Roles

THE ADMINISTRATIVE SUB-SYSTEM

The administrative sub-system has two major functions. First, it mediates between the school system as a whole and the broader society of which the school system is a part. Second, it directs the achievement of the school's goals. In this capacity it coordinates and plans the ways goals may best be achieved and supervises the processes involved in goal achievement.

Social Mediation Roles of School Administration. A number of administrative roles have been developed in large school systems to mediate between the school and society.

The key role in mediation belongs to the *superintendent.* As the administrative head of the school system, the superintendent is responsible for seeing that the system receives enough energy input, primarily in the form of money, to keep the system operating and achieving its goals.

The superintendent is selected by the board of education in

each school district. Members of the board are usually elected by the citizens of the district. The superintendent meets with the board of education regularly and acts as its professional advisor in setting policy and in communicating and interpreting the needs of the school system to the community.

The superintendent is constantly involved in what is best termed public relations activities. He is mainly responsible for casting the image of the school as perceived by the community. In order to do so, he often speaks to civic groups and usually belongs to a number of social organizations. He may also play a central role in community activities such as the Community Chest drive and other charitable causes. The success of the school system's money input is often determined by the image and personality of the superintendent and his ability to communicate clearly and forcibly to the community and to the board of education.

Most school systems today have a *business manager* who also has a role in mediating between the school and the society. The business manager is not ordinarily a professional educator but a trained accountant or business executive. As a mediator, the business manager, in consultation with other administrators, prepares the budget requests which are submitted to the board of education for approval. The skill with which this budget is prepared and presented can have considerable impact on its acceptance or rejection by the board.

Another mediator between school and society is the *personnel director*, who is responsible for filling the sub-system roles with qualified persons. In order to do this, he must contact and often interview candidates. These candidates are most often located through state and university or college placement offices. The personnel director must contact and frequently visit these offices to discover and interview potential personnel for his school system. His ability to judge talent and to maintain good relationships with placement offices can be a crucial factor in the quality of persons attracted to the system.

A fourth mediation role is that of the *guidance coordinator*. Sometimes the director of personnel is also the director of guidance, but many times these functions are separated. The guidance coordinator must maintain close contact with many community organizations, such as social welfare agencies and psychiatric clinics. It is his responsibility to coordinate the school system's activities with those of individual students or the families of students.

Furthermore, the guidance role necessitates a concern for the output of the school system, i.e., the student. Guidance coordinators must be aware of the job opportunities and qualifications, and post-high school opportunities and requirements. With the help of other guidance personnel in the system, the guidance coordinator advises students on their academic programs and personal needs in terms of their future intentions, clarifies opportunities for graduates, administers tests and collects data on students for use in these functions, and generally keeps in contact with the broader society in relation to the product of the schools — student graduates.

Goal Achievement Roles of School Administration. A second major role of the administrative sub-system is that of goal achievement. Goal achievement roles are related to the direct facilitation of the purposes of the school. Although the primary goal of the schools is to produce educated persons, the purposes of the school

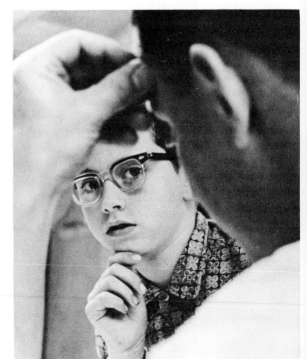

Many new materials are available which can help a teacher to accomplish his aims.

are not limited to student learning. Nevertheless, to produce educated persons, the best possible curriculum, sound instruction, and appropriately allocated resources are necessary. Furthermore, the three sub-systems must be maintained and coordinated. A number of specific roles have been developed for these purposes.

Today large school systems often have a *director of research.* This position may or may not be combined with or coordinated through either the curriculum coordinator (see below), the director of personnel, or the guidance coordinator. The director of research functions in two roles: (1) institutional research and (2) research and development of programs and processes within the school system.

Institutional research involves the collection of data for the school system with respect to the number of students enrolled in various grade levels, at which schools, and from what kinds of home environments, as well as the number of teachers in which schools, etc. Data concerning, for example, where graduates go, what they do, and how well they succeed may also be gathered.

The research and development role of the director of research relates to the generation and assessment of new programs and ideas which are to be carried out in the school system. Research and development programs are especially important in this age of federally supported programs for disadvantaged youth (Title I, Elementary and Secondary School Act) and innovation and dissemination activity (Title III of the same Act, discussed in Chapter Eight). Although the function of research and development is crucial for schools, school systems have not participated in this function to the extent that industry has. Industrial budgets may range up to as much as 10 per cent of total funds for research and development. Seldom, if ever, do school budgets include even as much as 1 per cent for the same purpose.

The *curriculum coordinator* is a second goal achievement role of school administration. Usually entitled "assistant superintendent," the curriculum coordinator is responsible for the development and implementation of curricular plans. In larger systems more than one curriculum coordinator may exist, each being responsible for only one educational level, i.e. elementary or secondary. It is his responsibility to organize school personnel for planning and to coordinate the supervision of the implementation of plans in instructional settings.

Planning activity requires that the curriculum coordinator bring to the staff outside resources in the form of consultants, new materials, new ideas, etc., and that he help the staff organize for the development of planning. Organizing for planning entails the making of decisions concerning the tasks that need to be accomplished (e.g., selecting new textbooks or developing new courses) and the processes by which such tasks will be accomplished (e.g., grade level teacher committees or school staff meetings).

The curriculum coordinator, in other words, is responsible for maintaining the quality of the educational program, and for the continuous analysis and improvement of this quality.

The implementation of plans involves the coordination of the plans throughout the school system and the supervision of the activities through which they are carried out. In order to do this, the curriculum coordinator usually has a staff of *supervisors*. He may also work directly with *building principals*. The supervisors may be subject specialists at the secondary level (e.g., English or physical education) or general supervisors (e.g., primary education, elementary education, or secondary education).

The common role expectations of supervisors (and building principals when they supervise) are to oversee and help with the implementation of curriculum plans in instructional settings and to assist the curriculum coordinator in developing the curriculum.

Supervisors operate in two general ways. They often visit teachers to assess their needs and to give help in the classroom; they also assist the coordinator by organizing and leading curriculum committees and groups in the school system in the development of plans. Supervisors may or may not be involved in the evaluation of teachers for such purposes as merit pay recommendations, dismissal, or recommendations for tenure. Such functions, when performed by supervisors, become a form of quality control in implementing the instructional program. When these evaluations are not made by supervisors, the building principal or perhaps department chairmen (in large high schools) will perform this quality assessment.

The building principal and any assistants he may have play what might be called a "minor league game" of superintending. The principal is the administrative contact between the school and the system. He prepares the school budget, allocates materials and resources to various classrooms, coordinates the school program through scheduling, advising, and supervising. He meets with and represents the school to parents and the community, advises the central administration with respect to over-all school policy as it pertains to his situation, and maintains good working relationships among his staff members.

To accomplish these tasks adequately the principal normally requires a competent *school secretary*. The school secretary relieves the principal of routine chores, freeing him for the more important tasks requiring professional competency. The secretary will often handle parental phone calls, keep school records, and coordinate the actual allocation of materials and facilities (such as duplicating machines) for individual teachers.

The administrative sub-system also includes non-professional maintenance personnel. Often a supervisor of buildings and grounds or maintenance exists with a crew or crews of workers, who see to the upkeep of the physical facilities of the school system. Each school usually has one or more custodians (or janitors), under the supervision of either the principal or the chief supervisor of maintenance, to look after the details of building cleanliness, upkeep, heating, and other necessities.

The administistative sub-system is usually characterized by line authority relationships. Thus, the organization chart of the school administration may resemble the one shown in Figure 5. This chart does not represent the only lines of authority possible; many variations occur throughout the school systems of our country.

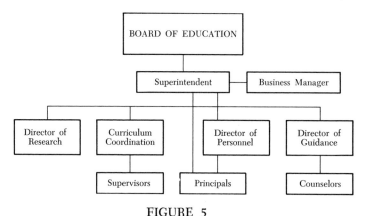

FIGURE 5

Line Authority Relationships in School Administration

The Curriculum Development Sub-System

Many of the role players and some of the functions of the curriculum development sub-system have already been identified in the description of the administrative sub-system. It is well to keep in mind, however, the multi-role nature of school personnel. This characteristic is especially true of the curriculum development sub-system.

This sub-system is under the coordination of the curriculum director and his staff of supervisors and principals and includes from time to time most, if not all, of the teachers in the system. Whereas the major role of these persons as members of the administrative sub-system is to maintain and assess the quality of the instructional program, as members of the curriculum development sub-system they are primarily concerned with the development and implementation of plans. Thus, in the curriculum development sub-system, the emphasis shifts from school personnel, the primary focus of the administrative sub-system, to student learning.

The major tasks of curriculum development involve products, processes, and the involvement of school personnel in these processes and productions. These tasks are carried out through the creation of certain activities in the school system. One general function concerns *in-service education*. In-service education may refer to a variety of system activities developed to provide teachers (and others) with experiences which will improve their understanding and skill in curriculum development and instruction.

In its most oblique form, in-service education may encourage additional professional studies at a nearby college or university, perhaps leading to an advanced degree. But more generally it refers to special classes or activities developed by the school system to provide teachers those learning experiences which relate to clearly identified local curriculum or instructional needs.

The administrators involved (identified in the previous section) must know and assess the general status of the school program. They must then suggest or organize (often with the help and advice of teachers) the kinds of goals (or products) and processes necessary to improve the programs.

The teachers involved, depending upon the situation, take on the role of learners and participants in processes which produce

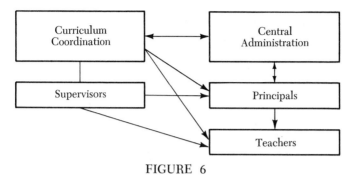

FIGURE 6

*Staff Authority Relationships in Curriculum
Development Sub-Systems*

the needed materials or techniques as specified either singly by
the administration or jointly with teachers.

Products and processes in the curriculum development sub-system vary widely. They might be oriented simply toward a change
in the attitudes of teachers toward students brought about through
the process of small monthly group discussions with human development experts. Or they might involve the large-scale production
of an entire social studies course produced over a two-year period
by teacher committees.

The curriculum development sub-system may best be thought
of as that aspect of the school system which maintains an adult
education focus whereby the leaders are playing teacher and
scholar roles. Teacher participation is crucial in this sub-system,
since, in the long run, the implementation of plans is almost completely dependent upon the teaching staff.

The roles of the curriculum development sub-system usually
have staff authority relationships, as illustrated in Figure 6, in
contrast to the line authority relationships of the administrative
sub-system roles. Thus authority in the curriculum development
sub-system is not normally exercised in a direct chain of command. The curriculum development roles are usually advisory
and ancillary to the direct line administrative relationships. In
one sense the curriculum development sub-system reflects a program service to the administrative sub-system. Changes in programs are usually not imposed on teachers and principals unless

the central administration incorporates these changes into a line order. Without this support the curriculum role players must encourage change through reason, stimulation, help, and support.

THE INSTRUCTIONAL SUB-SYSTEM

Each classroom (or class if departmentalized) is a separate social sub-system within the instructional sub-system. The classroom or class has two types of roles: *teacher* and *learner*. No two classes or classrooms are the same, since the introduction of new or different role players (usually different groups of students) changes the subtle social dynamics of the classroom.

The instructional sub-system is "where the action is" in the sense that the implementation of curricular plans, the quality of school programs, the service to the community and nation are embodied in the events which take place in the classroom.

The teacher is the social agent of the school system in the instructional sub-system. The teacher's role is focused on providing the best possible learning experiences for the students. The student's role in the instructional sub-system is to internalize the subject matter taught and to take maximum advantage of the learning opportunities provided in these situations.

One of the least discussed or least realized facets of schooling is that of the student role. Students are often thought of as "raw material" for schools rather than as role players in the school, yet the school cannot achieve its purposes unless the students take on the appropriate role behavior. Evidence of chaos and confusion are obvious when students do not live up to the expectations of their roles.

This is clearly demonstrated in situations in which student values learned in the home are in conflict with school curriculum expectations. Generally speaking, a student must defer to the teacher as the initiator of activity and as the source of authority in the classroom. Furthermore, he must often delay the satisfaction of immediate interests for the sake of long-range school goals. He is also expected to be attentive, follow directions, work hard, and follow the rules of social interaction which are either developed by the group or by the teacher.

Thus, when a classroom is composed of a number of students who do not pay attention, who threaten the teacher's control of the class, who refuse to do assigned work or even to follow directions, and who follow peer group norms (or others) rather than teacher–school norms, very little "teaching" can take place. In this sort of situation, the students either have not learned or will not learn to function according to the rules of the school "game." Regardless of why they will not, it is clear that they do not do so.

When circumstances such as these arise the school may regard them in four general ways: (1) The school (and teacher) may modify the content of the curriculum to a point where student interest and concern are captured and the students begin to "play the school game"; (2) a special class or curriculum may be developed which attempts to segregate and thus control such students; (3) the students may be expelled; and (4) the students may be referred for psychological testing and help.

What should be clear in all this is that children from low socio-economic backgrounds do not "naturally" fit into the roles of our middle class schools. On the other hand, individual youngsters from the middle class (or any class) may have crippling personality problems which interfere with role playing. In either case, regardless of cause, the effect is a disruption of the classroom because of the failure or inability of certain students to play productive school roles.

Beyond these obvious circumstances, many "normal" students have not grasped, been taught, or learned the subtleties of being a "good" student. Thus, there are ways of studying that are more productive than others; there are test-taking approaches that maximize success; and there are interpersonal nuances that make a difference in role playing.

In the long run, we may hope that students will opt for learning, per se, and see their taking on of student role behavior as an effective way to facilitate learning; but for those who do not, we may at least hope that they and their teachers are aware of their role expectations, and that they may have the option of deliberately choosing to play or not to play.

In the instructional sub-system the teacher is expected to assume responsibility for implementing curricular plans. This involves a wide variety of abilities and skills and requires considerable knowledge. One central aspect of the teaching role involves the *presentation of information and ideas to students*. Broadly speaking, this function may be characterized as putting the student in contact with significant subject matter. The teacher may accomplish this purpose through lectures, assigned readings, programmed learning, films, and closed-circuit television. The teacher may put the students in contact with vital information and useful ideas by inviting resource persons into the classroom or by taking the class to special resource persons or places. He may also use discussions, small group projects, and individual study in the process. It should be obvious that a teacher must know a great deal about subject matter and resources for learning to perform this function competently.

Another significant instructional role of the teacher is *mediation between curriculum plans and students.* The teacher is expected to know the kinds of students he has in his classes well enough to stimulate the best possible involvement of students in school work. Thus, he must be qualified to make decisions regarding variations in the scope, sequence, and quantity of material dealt with as he creates and adjusts the maximum conditions for learning in relation to the past experiences, abilities, and aspirations of the specific students in a class.

A third important function of the teacher concerns the knowledge and skill with which he *plans and creates the specific classroom environment.* The teacher is expected to know what materials and resources are available to help achieve the goals of the schools; he is expected to know what kinds of activities will best serve these goals; and he is expected to be able to create the kind of social climate and interaction that will best facilitate the learning process.

These three teacher roles — putting students in contact with subject matter, mediating between curriculum plans and students, and creating specific classroom conditions — are often seen in terms of the kinds of decisions teachers are called upon to make. The four major types of decisions are usually concerned with (1) instructional objectives, (2) the selection of learning experiences, (3) the organization of learning experiences, and (4) evaluation.[1]

[1] See Ralph Tyler, *Principles of Curriculum and Instruction* (Chicago: University of Chicago Press, 1950).

These girls are listening to a specially taped science program.

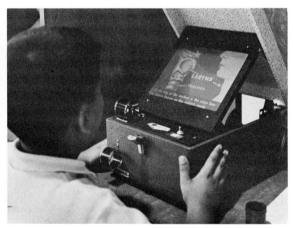

A student studies a film strip on a special viewer in a study carrel.

These high school boys are learning to use computers.

The question of *what* to teach is related both to the curriculum plans and the specific students. The teacher must be able to select from broad school purposes and subject-matter area goals a set of specific *instructional objectives* which he will pursue with a given class.

Further, once goals are clarified, the teacher must be able to select *learning experiences* which will maximize the possibility of achieving these objectives. Usually these experiences are thought of in terms of activities. Some common school activities are reading, writing, speaking, listening, observing, planning, reporting, discussing, and experimenting.

The question of *how* to teach also involves the organization of experiences over a period of time and the correlation of experiences at any given time. Thus, teachers must make decisions about the *sequence* of activities over time and the *relationship of activities* in subject areas at any given time. In this connection, for example, awareness of such a simple matter as variety in activities over a period of time can be of great importance.

A fourth area in which teachers must make decisions is *evaluation*. How to evaluate, when to evaluate, and how to use evaluation data to improve learning and teaching are important decision problems in teaching. The teacher must have considerable knowledge regarding testing (e.g., construction, administration, scoring, and using results). He must also recognize and correctly interpret signs of success and failure in the decisions he has made.

In essence the teacher role is one of the most complex and difficult social roles in our society. It demands great sensitivity to people, broad knowledge of subject matter, considerable awareness of resources, materials, and conditions that will facilitate learning, skill in working with groups, and great flexibility in personal behavior.

Role Fulfillment and Performance

ACHIEVEMENT AND ASCRIPTION

In our society we are prone to think that role fulfillment is achieved through hard work, talent, and opportunity. This is only partially true, however. Role fulfillment possesses elements of both achievement and ascription, since some roles are more nearly filled by being ascribed in terms of characteristics of the persons filling them.

The school reflects our broader cultural situation. Although it is very rare to find clear-cut cases of pure ascription in the school, there are many instances where one may suspect some element of it in operation. Ascription to roles is in one way a form of prejudice. That is, when access to roles is systematically denied a group of people, we often find a prejudicial attitude involved. Only when ascription is so culturally basic that it seems "natural" are we unaware of the attitudinal variance in terms of personal characteristics.

Age and sex are two basic characteristics that are almost universally related to ascribed role expectations. Thus, it is not surprising that we may find evidence of it in schools. We shall look first at students, then staff members, and finally the general school policies to see how they are related to the filling of roles in relation to age, sex, and other characteristics. Roles are, we must restate, seen as expectations of people in relation to their characteristics (ascribed qualities) or performances (achieved).

Students are generally not expected to make important decisions regarding their education. There is, further, greater expectation of the need for control at younger ages. Thus, we may say that the student role is ascribed and that there are variations in expectations at different age levels.

There is also considerable data which suggest that the sex of students is a meaningful characteristic in expectations of performance, either directly or indirectly. Thus, although there are no significant differences in intelligence between boys and girls, most studies show, for example, that boys represent about 75 per cent of the stutterers, 70 to 80 per cent of the behavior problems, 70 to 80 per cent of the slow readers, and a large majority of the dropouts in later school years.

There are obvious cultural and perhaps biological factors beyond the school that are reflected in these data. Still, the role expectations of boys are not exactly the same as those for girls, and these expectations are noticeable in systematic variances in expectations of performance, social behavior, grades, interests, and motivation.

Other personal characteristics of students are sometimes used to ascribe roles to individuals. Thus, expectations of students identified as talented or gifted vary from those characterized as slow learners and/or behavior problems. Recognition of this fact may be focused in many places where grouping for instruction by those characteristics is practiced. Even within single classrooms or classes it is not uncommon to find certain individuals whose characteristics find ascribed status such as "teacher's helper," "errand boy," etc.

Today many sociologists and educators are concerned about the ascription of roles to culturally different children. Although poor children perform significantly less well as a group than most youngsters in our society, there is apparently some danger of crystallizing expectations for these children and thus trapping them in a role expectation that might preclude whatever chance they have to achieve.

Getzels and Jackson have noted a very special case of school-developed role expectations in their study of creative students.[2] They found that among students of equal achievement, those classified as creative (in comparison with those classified by I.Q. as intelligent) were perceived differently by teachers and that they perceived the school situation differently. The results of this study showed that teachers clearly preferred the highly intelligent student over the highly creative student, even though their achievement was the same. Further, the highly creative students' perception of possible careers and teachers differed from those of the highly intelligent students. These characteristics of highly creative students placed them in a role context in schools that differentiated them from others, and these "role" behaviors were known by teachers and students alike.

Staff roles are also only partially achieved in many cases. Thus, it is rare (in proportion to the numbers of persons in the profession) for women to be selected for administrative positions. Indeed, it is almost unheard of for a woman to become a superintendent of schools. Men, on the other hand, are rarely allowed to teach below the third or fourth grade level.

[2] Jacob W. Getzels and Philip W. Jackson, *Creativity and Intelligence* (New York: John Wiley & Sons, 1962).

The age of staff members also causes a differential expectation that probably is not due to other factors. Thus, in a profession in which seniority is the basis for tenure and pay increases, other expectations accrue with age. Younger persons, say, less than thirty years old, often may find it difficult to achieve responsible roles regardless of talent until they are seasoned by age. Again, this is not a pure case of ascription, but it does have elements of it.

Thus, in a loose way, career women "work their way up" in the school organization from teaching to supervising. Some go on to college teaching. Men, on the other hand, move from teaching to a principalship, to guidance or personnel work and superintendencies or on to college teaching in much larger proportions. And it is still not uncommon to find differential pay scales, although often these are justified by armed service credit for men or "added responsibilities" of a minor nature.

The general policies of the school system may add to or minimize the development of ascribed roles for both students or staff members. College preparatory curriculum plans will usually result in differentiating students of high and low socioeconomic class status, with a resultant variation in role expectations for most students in each group. Standardized testing programs help this process by providing numerical cut-off points and "new" sets of characteristics by which status and role expectations may be developed and allotted.

The hiring and assignment practices of school systems are also open to some ascription of roles by age, sex, and class and sometimes by race and religious and ethnic background. It is almost impossible to document this kind of ascription in relation to hiring, but evidence of it can be seen in the practice of many large school systems of assigning Negro teachers to predominantly Negro schools, and/or assigning the youngest teachers to the "toughest" situations. Furthermore, teachers who are hired by affluent suburban communities are often noticeably more "higher class" in subtle language usage, dress, and mannerisms.

In summary, then, the filling of roles in the schools is not clearly a matter of achievement. There is evidence, both among staff and student roles, of differential assignment or ascription on the basis of group qualities or characteristics, some of which predominate in the larger society as well, and some which seem to be part of the traditional culture of the schools.

The Relationship Between Personality and Role

Roles must be performed adequately, regardless of how they are allotted and regardless of the personalities filling them. Otherwise, the school system cannot maintain itself or achieve its intended goals. However, the school system will be unable to maintain itself if, on the other hand, roles are assigned without regard for achievement, or are so restrictive that most persons cannot fit comfortably into them. Consequently, most roles are somewhat flexible and partial role redefinition and variation are acceptable; each person may have his own special talent and expressive style when filling roles in the various sub-systems of the school.

Jourard and Overlade have identified four "talent flairs" that are useful in indicating the relationships between personalities and role playing.[3] Some persons are fascinated with the problem of conceptualization. Such persons characteristically are thinkers who have *interpretive* talent. Others are more interested in problems of manipulating power and have *political* talent. Still other persons (such as engineers and actors) like problems that deal with putting ideas into practice. Their talent may be called *technological*. Finally, there are individuals who are most concerned with the performance of other persons and have what may be termed *humanistic* talent.

A teacher, for example, may perform best when he is contriving creative plans for instruction (interpretive), or managing the classroom and maintaining discipline (political), or "covering" the curriculum and getting things done (technological), or creating warm human relationships and encouraging pupil growth (humanistic). All of these talent flairs are useful and acceptable within the general role structure of teaching. Each person will have some talent in each area, but possibly more in one direction than in the others.

Some school system roles seem to need at least a minimum of

[3] Sidney Jourard and D. C. Overlade, eds., *Reconciliation Theory* (New York: D. Van Nostrand Co. [Insight Books], 1966).

The multi-role responsibilities of persons in schools can also cause friction and conflict. Thus, when teachers are asked to participate in in-service education and curriculum development activities, the resulting loss of time for preparation for teaching can cause tension and feelings of anxiety. Principals may also develop frustrations when the pressures of the administrative subsystem produce activity which in effect minimizes the role of the principal in supervision and curriculum development. Thus, some principals live with guilt feelings when they are not able to meet the total role expectations of their positions.

Some persons are simply not suited to their positions. Thus, teachers, for example, who have little patience or are generally hostile toward others may be unhappy in their instructional role, or may be assessed as inadequate for teaching. Considerable friction and conflict between staff members can often be caused by individuals who simply are unsuited to their role expectations in the school system. Schools have not solved this problem with any great success, since early identification of problems is difficult and tenure and other policies make dismissal a painful procedure.

The Organizational Climate

The total organizational climate and the policies of the system have a direct and dramatic effect on the way persons feel about themselves in their roles, and the degree of conflict potential existing in the school system.

When the specific school system is characterized by rigid lines of authority which are tenaciously maintained, by numerous operating policies which are actively imposed, and by hierarchical communication patterns which are clearly specified and limiting, then the amount of leeway in role playing is severely reduced.

Evidence of a highly controlled school organization may be found, for example, in a teacher's perception of the necessity to adhere to a specific curricular plan and schedule at all costs; or in a principal's inability or lack of desire to take the initiative in implementing new programs or proposals, or in a generally restrictive climate of personality and bureaucratic control. Systems organized in such ways do not provide optimum conditions for staff members to be creative or to grow, even though they may be highly efficient and effective in achieving their goals.

acting. Our search, then, must include seeking those who "feel with" us on life's major commitments and, more importantly, seeking those who will "act with" us in striving to achieve a common goal. Yet how often have we seen the truth of the aphorism, "One man with courage is a majority." Today, in a world in which the increasing proximity of all men to all others is an incontrovertible fact, it is easy to lose oneself in the commitments of others. To stand alone in opinion or commitment is often to stand alone socially. The "courage to be" of which Tillich has written is difficult enough, but the courage to be *and act* in the fervent hope that one's actions will bring forth responses in others who have been groping and faltering is the most difficult yet noble human undertaking. Various philosophers have stated this in many ways: "Do unto others . . ."; "so act [that your actions may be] . . . universal law"; "a man cannot help others without also helping himself."

To act in any other way is to be existentially immoral. All we have is each other, and no one is strong enough to "go it alone" in all the situations of living. We need the unique strengths, broadly defined, of all of us to meet the countless perils and difficulties of life. And "strength," as we use it here, may be knowledge, skills, physical prowess, sympathetic listening and encouragement, creative talents, etc. Strengths are as broad as the range of human possibilities; one never knows when a particular form of strength will be needed, or who can best supply it at a given time to a given fellow man.

The Teacher's Value-Charged Position

The teacher is in a particularly value-charged position, not only because both law and parents entrust the ductile personalities and minds of children to the teacher, but also because the tap root of commitment formation lies before him. It is true that peer groups, parents, and mass media often play a larger part in value formation than do educators, but this situation is an "is," not necessarily an "ought" of our society. Each of these influences has its own value-commitment patterns to "sell" to youth, and in varying degrees each may have the welfare of the child in mind — but only in terms of the goals and worldview important to the

Chapter Ten

RELEVANCE IN
THE MODERN WORLD

The many problems and trends discussed in the foregoing chapters may seem overwhelming to the teacher candidate or to the newly employed teacher. The complex phenomena such as alienation, value conflicts, role changes, and the search for an understanding of the implications of the social sciences for education cry out for action. The individual teacher, however, who often finds his situation lonely and frustrating, may wonder "What can I do? I am only one person."

Senancour once wrote, "It is said that no other fate awaits us except the nothingness of death. That may be; but let us *perish resisting*, so that if that be so, it shall be an unjust fate." This wise and courageous observation is particularly apropos today. It offers no magic solutions; it promises no rewards to come. It merely states that whatever meaning we may find in our lives we must put there by our actions; that, in the final analysis, we may never know the results of our existence, but we must act in some way, for that is what it is to live. As Sartre says, "Choosing not to choose is itself a choice."

Although we combine our actions when we seek to serve common commitments, even then we are a collection of *individuals*

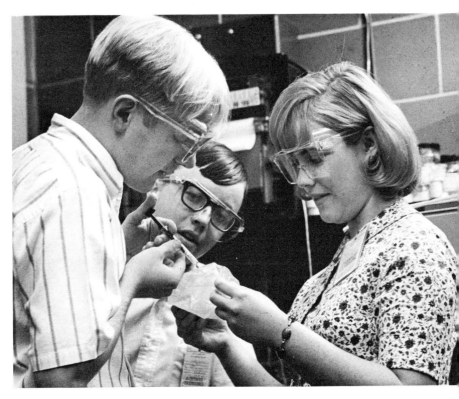

High school students attend a three-day workshop at a Du Pont textile plant.

PART FOUR

Education for Relevance

[Educational philosophy for the future] will be a philosophy of culture, with education conceived as the chief agency through which problems of every kind are attacked, and practices, institutions, and values commensurate with the demands of the emerging age are developed and tested.

THEODORE BRAMELD

Gordon, C. Wayne. *The Adolescent Society*. New York: Free Press of Glencoe, 1961.

Gross, Neil, W. S. Mason, and A. W. McEachern. *Explorations in Role Analysis: Studies of the School Superintendency Role*. New York: John Wiley & Sons, 1958.

Hodgkinson, Harold L. *Education, Interaction, and Social Change*. Englewood Cliffs, N.J.: Prentice-Hall, 1967.

Waller, Willard. *The Sociology of Teaching*. New York: John Wiley & Sons, 1937.

Young, Michael. *The Rise of Meritocracy*. Baltimore: Penguin Books, 1961.

of organization (for example, whether highly rigid and bureaucratic or loosely controlled and democratic) will create working conditions that affect the kinds of decisions made throughout the system. Further, the skill with which the system is managed will be felt at all levels.

The kinds of curricular plans developed also affect learning to a great extent. Thus, plans that are poorly thought through and poorly coordinated and are not based on the best sources of knowledge are obviously of less value than well made curricular plans. The procedures for developing plans and the form that plans take are also important. For example, if teachers are not involved in planning in some way there appears to be little chance that the plans can be intelligently implemented in instruction. And plans that are highly rigid or abstract are not as accessible to teachers as plans that are less rigid and abstract.

The instructional (classroom) level, where plans are implemented and supervised in teaching–learning situations can render even the best plans and resources of little value if the quality of instruction is poor. Just as instruction is dependent on resources and plans, both are equally dependent upon intelligent implementation and use in order to achieve system goals. Thus, the interaction and role playing of teachers, students, principals, and supervisors is extremely important. The exercise of authority, the manner and channels of communication, and the knowledge, techniques, and attitudes of the role players will create practices and climates that can dramatically affect the learned outcomes.

What is learned, then, is a result of a very complex interaction of multiple roles and personal characteristics. No one element or person is necessarily more important than another. Each person in the sub-systems is highly dependent upon the activity and roles of others. Each role player has the responsibility of seeing his role and functioning in terms of the total system.

SUGGESTIONS FOR FURTHER READING

Goffman, Irving. *The Presentation of Self in Everyday Life.* Garden City, N.Y.: Doubleday & Company, 1959.

Recent evidence from the study of economic organizations such as banks, factories, and department stores suggests that the efficiency of highly controlled organizations is a myth of classical economic theory. Studies[4] indicate that complex organizations have a number of purposes which sometimes conflict and that these conflicts often cause different segments of the organizations to work at cross purposes. They also indicate that attempts to control the sub-systems of a complex organization by rigid policies may very well contribute to the inefficiency and ineffectiveness they were designed to reduce.

Review of Factors Affecting Goal Achievement

The goal achievement of the school system is seen primarily in terms of the things students know and can do as a result of their experience in the school. It should be clear that there are many factors which influence these outcomes.

These influences can be grouped into two large categories (as suggested earlier): (1) the nature of the social system (as seen in the functions of role expectations) and (2) the quality of the persons filling roles.

The quality of the persons who staff our schools can affect student learning in myriad ways. The ability of the superintendent to project an image of competence into the community, to shape policy and manage the system, and to communicate the needs and goals of the system is crucial. However, no less crucial are the qualities of teachers, their knowledge, skill, commitments, and attitudes. Each staff member, in other words, will affect the system in some manner by the kind of personal characteristics, flair, and style that he brings to his role playing in the system. Of course, the characteristics students bring to their roles also have a great effect upon the system.

Beyond this, however, the social arrangements themselves have a powerful influence upon the learning outcomes. Thus, the type

[4] See James March, "Organizational Factors in Supervision," in *The Supervisor: Agent for Change in Teaching*, ed. James Raths (Washington: National Education Association, Association for Supervision and Curriculum Development 1966), pp. 107–124.

Education
for Relevance

[Educational philosophy for the future] will be a
philosophy of culture, with education conceived
as the chief agency through which problems
of every kind are attacked, and practices,
institutions, and values commensurate with
the demands of the emerging age are developed
and tested.

THEODORE BRAMELD

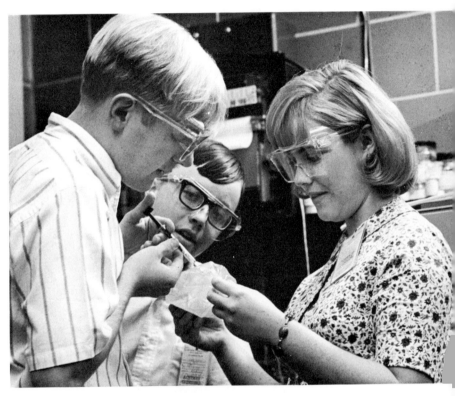

High school students attend a three-day workshop at a Du Pont textile plant.

Chapter Ten

RELEVANCE IN
THE MODERN WORLD

The many problems and trends discussed in the foregoing chapters may seem overwhelming to the teacher candidate or to the newly employed teacher. The complex phenomena such as alienation, value conflicts, role changes, and the search for an understanding of the implications of the social sciences for education cry out for action. The individual teacher, however, who often finds his situation lonely and frustrating, may wonder "What can I do? I am only one person."

Senancour once wrote, "It is said that no other fate awaits us except the nothingness of death. That may be; but let us *perish resisting,* so that if that be so, it shall be an unjust fate." This wise and courageous observation is particularly apropos today. It offers no magic solutions; it promises no rewards to come. It merely states that whatever meaning we may find in our lives we must put there by our actions; that, in the final analysis, we may never know the results of our existence, but we must act in some way, for that is what it is to live. As Sartre says, "Choosing not to choose is itself a choice."

Although we combine our actions when we seek to serve common commitments, even then we are a collection of *individuals* acting. Our search, then, must include seeking those who "feel with" us on life's major commitments and, more importantly, seeking those who will "act with" us in striving to achieve a common goal. Yet how often have we seen the truth of the aphorism, "One man with courage is a majority." Today, in a world in which the increasing proximity of all men to all others is an incontrovertible fact, it is easy to lose oneself in the commitments of others. To stand alone in opinion or commitment is often to stand alone socially. The "courage to be" of which Tillich has written is difficult enough, but the courage to be *and act* in the fervent hope that one's actions will bring forth responses in others who have been groping and faltering is the most difficult yet noble human undertaking. Various philosophers have stated this in many ways: "Do unto others . . ."; "so act [that your actions may be] . . . universal law"; "a man cannot help others without also helping himself."

To act in any other way is to be existentially immoral. All we have is each other, and no one is strong enough to "go it alone" in all the situations of living. We need the unique strengths, broadly defined, of all of us to meet the countless perils and difficulties of life. And "strength," as we use it here, may be knowledge, skills, physical prowess, sympathetic listening and encouragement, creative talents, etc. Strengths are as broad as the range of human possibilities; one never knows when a particular form of strength will be needed, or who can best supply it at a given time to a given fellow man.

The Teacher's Value-Charged Position

The teacher is in a particularly value-charged position, not only because both law and parents entrust the ductile personalities and minds of children to the teacher, but also because the tap root of commitment formation lies before him. It is true that peer groups, parents, and mass media often play a larger part in value formation than do educators, but this situation is an "is," not necessarily an "ought" of our society. Each of these influences has its own value-commitment patterns to "sell" to youth, and in varying degrees each may have the welfare of the child in mind — but only in terms of the goals and worldview important to the

This Vista volunteer displays her willingness to "feel with" and help others. Vista, a domestic Peace Corps, sends volunteers to poor communities where they live and work with the people.

group itself. In effect, each is saying, "Here is what we stand for. We have some claim on you because you are somehow part of us. We want you to be more like us, to share what we value, to live as we think life ought to be lived."

What, then, does the teacher do, assuming that he decides to make a contribution, however small, toward stemming or slowing the tide of certain trends? This question presupposes two other important questions: (1) What trends or phenomena does the teacher feel deeply are in need of being slowed or reversed? and (2) What strengths does the teacher have or can he attain in order to contribute? Only when these two questions are answered can the one above be truly meaningful. We must therefore hold the latter in abeyance until later in this chapter.

Before we can answer the second two questions, however, we must note that any philosophy of education or any theory of educational change must deal with the vital historical questions from which all others derive: (1) Who shall learn? (2) Who shall teach? and (3) What shall be taught?

ARGUMENT BY PRECEDENT

Each society and many subcultures within them have provided answers from their own perspective. Most of the nations have written into law the opinion of the power structure on these matters. But law, too, is an "is," and not necessarily an "ought." Although a time-tested law ought to represent the best thinking of a group based on past experience and present problems, what ought to have been in the past becomes only an "is" in the present unless and until it has been re-examined and has won anew the right to present "oughtness." The legal profession recognizes this fact by providing methods, orderly and socially sanctioned, by which laws can be amended or replaced. The basic principles underlying statutes themselves are open to scrutiny and to redefinition. For example, one society begins with the assumption that a man charged with a crime is innocent until proved guilty, while other societies place the burden of proof upon the accused to show that he is *not* "guilty as charged." Clearly, both assumptions cannot be "right" and "true" in some ultimate, absolute sense and if even this basic presupposition is open to question, surely all individual laws must be reviewed often to determine their relevance to present-day living. Our "world in context" is the only world we can know directly, the only one in which we can live, and the only one in which any actions we may take will count for anything.

Argument by precedent is a dangerous approach to any serious problem involving large numbers of human beings. "Precedent," said the Houhynhym to Gulliver, "is making sure we always make the same mistake each time we are faced with like situations." We have all too long reacted in this way. It is a secure way, lacking no guidelines — and lacking any other redeeming virtue. The age of an action is no guarantee of its value in this situation today any more than there is a guarantee in saying Joe Louis *is* the greatest fighter alive because it once was true. Situations change, and actions go through an "aging" process as do human beings. The traditional view of morality, law, and other stabilizing influences is that they are timeless truths, applicable in all times in all situations for all men, and that all *other* things being *equal,* the time-tested answers to our problems of living together will be the ones to follow. But when are all other things ever equal? If a law or moral rule does apply in today's situation it is not because it is time-tested, but rather because it has been present-tested and found effective in moving us toward our chosen goal, whatever the nature of that goal might happen to be. A law, a moral edict, or other conduct guide *may* apply as well now as in past times, but let us be clear about why it does, and lay to rest once and for all the eternal rightness of precedent in conduct. A guide to conduct must prove itself *relevant* to the world in which we choose — by our actions — to live.

Indeed, "relevance" appears to be the unifying concept, the thread of continuity running through all of the previous chapters of this volume. Changes are made historically because older ways are no longer relevant; value changes take place because of the apparent irrelevance of previous values, or at least the degree of relevance found in past values; roles change as it becomes apparent that new or broader goals cannot be served by the roles as previously conceived; and alienation, taking several forms, is a result of some manner of irrelevance.

The teacher, then, must ask himself just how relevant, how pertinent, are his contributions and those of his subject matter to the lives of his students, and to the lives of others, both now and in the future. He must take seriously the *con*tent, if not always the *in*tent, of the perennial student lament, "Why do we have to know *this* stuff?" There is indeed much deadwood in the curriculum and within individual courses, and often it is the student rather than the instructor who first sees it and most openly expresses his displeasure with it. Yet no mature, knowledgeable teacher will strike out every curricular item which meets with student resistance, because even though the student himself is the one who must in the ultimate analysis be the judge of what is truly relevant in his life, he is often too close to the problem to see it clearly. He is too involved with his own ego protection and defenses, his own preferences and strengths, to judge fairly and quickly the relevance of material which he is only now confronting for the first time. But by the same reasoning, no teacher should dismiss such criticisms out of hand. For the teacher, too, and his colleagues, and those who first educated him for his position, have their own ego-protection and defense mechanisms at work. It is far more comfortable to keep teaching the things that have "always been taught," as was mentioned in Chapter One with regard to the amusing yet frightening *Saber-Tooth Curriculum.* This "clubbing of tigers" academically even after all of them are extinct is the nadir point in the concept of relevance.

RELEVANCE AND THE CURRICULUM

There are many serious cases of irrelevance still with us today. They typically rest on one of two bases. Either the teacher does not recognize that the matter is now irrelevant, if it ever was relevant, or he is unwilling to change, discard, or restructure his materials and procedures as relevance demands. In the latter situation, he is in effect viewing the school as remote from life, an ivory tower, a pleasant set of verbal gymnastics, or a sort of academic competitiveness which is somehow "right" to be practiced in and of itself, because tradition has so decreed it.

It is not enough to say of a given pet procedure that it "doesn't hurt anyone" to study it; the criterion should be, Does it help anyone? If the only person it helps is the teacher, by satisfying his need for dominance or feeding his vanity, then it would seem to be worse than useless, or to use a term previously employed in this discussion, "existentially immoral." Since we have only the time between life and death to define ourselves by our actions, it would appear a tragic misuse of the time of both teacher and student to pursue the hollowness of actions which "don't hurt anybody." Especially when the world is so full of things to be learned in every field of endeavor which can help us in our existential journey.

Of the two bases upon which irrelevance seems to rest, it would appear that knowingly pursuing the inertia-bound or comfort-oriented courses of action is the most serious. However, the consistent lack of knowledge of what is relevant to the lives of students can be just as devastating and just as unprofessional. In the professional preparation of teachers, and in our own continuing self-improvement within our chosen field, we must guard against *both* bases of irrelevance, for both are not only positive dangers to our effectiveness in the classroom, but both degrade us and our students by wasting our most precious existential commodity, time. One can do so much with time — or so little. No more striking statement of the preciousness of time in human existence is apt to be found in so few words than this one from Shakespeare: "I did waste time; now time doth waste me."

Let us be clear that this concern for time is *not* a call for stop-watch efficiency or time and motion studies in the classroom. In fact, we are a bit amused by all the current interest in the mathematics of interaction analysis in teaching situations. The word-count or talk-distribution of a student answering a question does not solve anything, or tell us anything, except in cases so gross that any casual observer could see it immediately. When asked to discuss the causes of some social or political event such as a given war, a student may speak cogently and correctly for many minutes — and still not understand the words he is using from texts he was forced to read on a subject he cares little about. No, top operating efficiency is not necessary. There is and must be time in the course of the day for contemplation, for mulling over, for speculating, for dreaming. Equally important as the psychologist's vaunted reality testing is perhaps the philosopher's fantasy testing. But both these practices should be purposeful and planned, not — as in the case of teaching the clubbing of "extinct tigers" — unplanned, purposeless, and wasteful of time.

It is the nature of a professional person that he works comparatively independently, that he makes judgments within his field of expertise, and that he upholds the pledge of good faith required of new members of most professions, whether overt or implied. It is also inevitable that unscrupulous "professionals" will be found in all fields. When these people are exposed for what they are, the field in which each operates is greatly benefited, but it is a sad fact that in teaching, a field some consider to be not yet a profession, many behaviors of a dubious nature are covered or smoke-screened by the cry of "academic freedom." Although academic freedom is the most important safeguard in our profession, we dare not allow it to become an all-encasing shield for malpractice, idleness, and ignorant behavior. The hallmark of any profession is the degree to which it performs the service it promises effectively and the degree to which such performance is self-policing. We cannot remain silent in the face of knowing malpractice on the part of members of our profession and remain true to our highest ideals. We must first try to work with and aid

"He will be unafraid to challenge old, time-honored ideas, both through his own personal efforts in the classroom and through his wider professional contacts."

our colleague, but if that fails, we must not rest until we have done all that is possible to restore whatever his ignorance, idleness, or inconsiderateness has brought about. Often it is not necessary to "air our academic dirty linen in public"; an erring or misdirected colleague is only too willing to redirect his efforts if only someone provides sound advice or other "strength" missing in his own training. Far better that the help come from a well-meaning colleague than from a hostile source which may wrongly interpret the moves of the "incompetent" or "perverse" teacher.

The teacher who is *secure enough as a person,* solid in his command of the basic structure and meaning of his disciplines, and alert to changes in his area of specialization and in related areas, will be unafraid of finding some irrelevance in his own work, or in having it pointed out to him, whether personally or by teachers of in-service courses. He will be unafraid to challenge old, time-honored ideas, both through his own personal efforts in the class-room and through his wider professional contacts. He will be unafraid to speak out in meetings, journals, in letters, through mass media, or organizations, or whatever means he deems best for the task at hand.

A major problem, then, is to produce teachers who are (1) secure as persons (presupposing adequate self-knowledge), (2) knowledgeable in their disciplines, (3) alert to changes (presupposing a knowledge of where to look for changes), (4) understanding of the learning process and of the learner, and (5) familiar with several alternative ways of teaching. No single teacher education institution can guarantee these minimal attainments, even though none would say any less than these are enough. Indeed, many current practices in teacher education institutions, as in all professional schools, may themselves prove to be irrelevant, although they are carried out in the name of these objectives. The pursuit of relevance must not be limited to any particular setting, for example, the classroom or the counseling office. It is a vital item for all who live and move in the educational milieu. It knows no sacred cows; it exempts no one from its effects.

Dangerous Trends and Combative Strengths

Now let us get back to the question of what a single teacher can do to make his teaching more relevant to the concerns of students, and to the two questions which necessarily precede this one, viz., What trends does the teacher deeply feel are in need of being slowed or reversed? and, What strengths does he now have or can he attain in order to do so?

Everyone's life has priorities or a hierarchy of competing "goods" or values, and there is no reason to feel that the teacher is an exception. He cannot and should not feel *deeply* about all causes, nor should he set about to attain all possible strengths necessary to set right all the evils of the world. There will be times when the teacher feels that he is standing quite alone, but the principle or trend he is fighting for or against is not unique to him. Others are involved in the same battle in other places, and the more vital the principle the more likely it is that other thinking people are involved with him in the attempt to reverse or slow the trend.

To return to the first "prior question" above, then, recent sociological and psychological studies have pointed out the dangers of and growing problems with several trends. Whether an individual teacher feels deeply enough about them to enter the arena must be an individual decision, but these warnings at least warrant the serious consideration of educators. Among these trends are the following:

1. Increasing impersonalization and bureaucratization of both schools and society.
2. Remaining inequalities of educational and economic opportunity.
3. Lack of commitment on the part of old and young alike.
4. Disregard for law and tradition with no substitute offered or sought.
5. The "lowering" of art forms, standards, and other culturemarks to an insipid "common denominator."
6. Pressures on both school and society from extremist political groups seeking imposition of certain goals not currently deemed desirable or "first priority" by educators.
7. Growing racial tensions and prejudiced actions.
8. Persistent international strife.
9. The outdistancing of moral and ethical developments by scientific development.
10. Revolts against the "old" morality with no viable substitutes offered.

This list is not intended to be comprehensive, but the cumulative effect of these problems has been to place the teacher and his students in a strange new situation where words often sound hollow, where feelings which (historically) "ought" to be deep are shallow, and where guidelines, such as they are, are most *unclear* when relevant and *quite* clear when irrelevant. (The latter phenomenon has been termed by other writers as "the dead hand of the past.") Strained relationships between student and teacher and among staff members are often traceable to this cumulative effect.

Let us now examine the other "prior question," What strengths does the individual teacher have or can he attain in order to contribute?

As previously stated, "strengths," broadly interpreted, can mean a great number of things almost inclusive of all the range of human possibilities in action. It can mean positive rapport, excellence in methods, expert knowledge in various aspects of subject matter, a well-timed aphorism, respect for students, special talents which suddenly "bridge" the other differences between teacher and student, and countless skills and abilities.

It must be noted that an individual student may suddenly find meaning in his life and/or in his school work by coming into contact with a teacher who exhibits unexpectedly a particular strength which fills in the space in his existential quandary. At this point, perhaps, a theoretical model might clarify the strength concept as it is used here to apply to all helping relationships, of which teaching — however vitally important — is only one.

The Helping Relationship

A famous nuclear physicist once wrote, in trying to extend Einstein's theory of relativity, "In every universe there must be a minimum of two particles — for the sake of energy exchange, and for establishing points of reference." The physicist's concern, of course, was with physical universes, but helping relationships, such as counseling and teaching, can also be viewed as a "universe of two." Even in a classroom full of students, each teacher–student interplay or interpretation is a separate universe of two, a relatedness which has a quality all its own and a spatial–temporal quality unlike that of any other student–teacher relationship simply because the component "particles" are different. This concept may be illustrated by the following diagram:

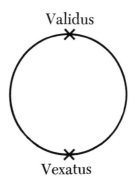

Validus

Vexatus

VEXATUS–VALIDUS

Let us label the two "particles" or persons as the "strength seeker" and the "strength source," or *vexatus* and *validus,* the

Latin equivalents meaning the "troubled one" and the "strong one." Note that the terms are situational, not static. Thus, *in this situation* (or "universe") the strong one, or *validus*, is viewed by the troubled one (*vexatus*) as either a source of some sort of strength that the *vexatus* participant does not have or does not know he has, or as one who can establish "points of reference" by acting as a sympathetic listener or by helping to synthesize his "position" in this and/or other situations. Here the teacher is typically cast in the *validus* role by most students in this situation (viz., teaching), i.e., the student acknowledges that the teacher has superior knowledge of subject matter, grants that he is older, has met learning problems before, etc. In summary, the teacher is one who can *reasonably* be expected to provide certain strengths in the form of knowledge, skills, etc., and can reasonably be expected to provide points of reference, e.g., clarification of student progress in the learning of new material. As mentioned above, the *vexatus–validus* situation is exactly that — *situational*. Perhaps in no other situation would this particular student view this particular older human being as being a strength source *to him*. Further acquaintance may prove otherwise, such as when the student may encounter the teacher later on a softball field in a student–faculty game and find to his amazement that the "strength source" in algebra is also a strength source in giving tips on how to throw an outcurve. But we are here concerned primarily with setting up a model for the teaching situation as it occurs typically in classrooms. We have stated that the teacher *reasonably* can be expected to have certain strengths, but this does not assure his students that he has them. Only performance will do this. Just as in the medical "helping relationship," where the doctor's prescription is assumed to be effective, only the actual taking of the medicine by *this* patient in *this* situation will prove whether the original assumption was accurate.

In medicine a doctor who finds that he does not have the particular strength required in the form of knowledge or technique usually refers the patient to someone else who can reasonably be expected to know more (the reference point idea). Or a patient who becomes dissatisfied with the fumbling and seemingly trial-and-error attempts of his physician may choose to leave this universe of two and refer his problem to someone else, who may or may not come closer to effective treatment than the original doctor. In education we have a similar situation. Although there may be the presumption of the strength and reference abilities of the teacher, it may be most erroneous indeed in relation to a given child. But the difference between this and the medical situation is that the child has no real recourse, for he and the teacher are "stuck" with each other for a semester, a year, or perhaps longer. Some teachers, lacking the security as persons which we have previously seen as being so important, may not admit, even to themselves, that the *vexatus–validus* model just does not prove out in relationships with a given student who is not learning, and who may begin to cause all sorts of other problems. If such a teacher would remember, however, that these roles are situational and not static, he might better be able to accept his ineffectiveness in this one situation. Of course, if the situation repeats itself frequently and severely, then the teacher may very correctly assume that his certificate to teach means little except a long, frustrating day, and unhappy, unlearning students. In other words, he has not sufficient breath or depth in the types of strength needed in many situations.

If he intends to continue in teaching, he would do well to examine himself and his knowledge right away. But he should feel no shame at doing this. No one can have strength in every situation, and this is true of students as well as teachers, of course. The boy who cannot grasp factoring in a math class may be quite able to find the mechanical trouble in the teacher's car at a garage where he works after school. The student — every student — has *validus* and *vexatus* times in certain situations. It is not the task of the teacher to make him "meet standards" in all situations, but rather to play to the strengths of the student whenever possible to build confidence, to allow the self-concept to move from an "I can't" toward an "I can" mentality.

The truly professional teacher is the one who will find ways to teach as much as he can in his field which is relevant to the lifestyle the student seems apt to lead. And the teacher must be ready to write off some students as — for them — unreachable, because no teacher can have enough strengths to reach every student who comes before him. He cannot be therapist, father, mentor, and sounding board to all students, especially in the relatively limited time of the school year. He must accept this fact as one of the sad but inevitable "givens" of teaching. Just as no doctor can cure all ills, neither can one teacher right the ravages of years of mistreatment in all mistreated children, or remedy the poor understandings of subjects and of life which took years to misconstrue. It may be that forces stronger than the strongest teacher are at work within some students, and there should be no feeling of humiliation in admitting that one cannot be all things to all men, or that one may fail sometimes.

LENDING STRENGTHS AND BUILDING STRENGTHS

In the model above it should be noted that *building* strength is deemed far better than *lending* strength, but because of time limitations and the press of circumstances we often must settle for a form of strength lending rather than strength building. For example, a teacher could in a math class teach a student to solve square root problems, and this might be relevant to some operation the student is likely to perform in his chosen field of endeavor. He may not understand the method the first time, so the teacher may try still another way to show him (building strength); but if the teacher exhausts his methods of "showing how," he may end up by merely tossing the boy a square root table and telling him to use it whenever he has problems of this sort (lending strength, i.e., not adding to the potential reserve of the student's own responses directly, but providing a crutch which may aid in problem solving).

There are many who would argue that the presentation of the square root table at the onset would take the pressure off the learning situation, and that even those who can do square root problems prefer to use tables for accuracy and speed. Thus the rule of thumb that it is preferable to build strength rather than to "lend" it may be inapplicable in some situations or semantically entangled in others.

THE TEACHER'S PRIMARY RESPONSIBILITY

The point of this model, and of the whole discussion of the "prior questions," was to build toward the key question previously posed, What can the teacher *do* about the trends which seem to present problems too difficult for him to solve alone?

Teachers are now taking positions on contemporary issues as a professional group.

If we assume that strength is situational, any sort of strength, then we must direct the teacher to examine himself, to take inventory of his strong points and of his weaknesses. It is not easy to face oneself in this way at times, but it is necessary and sensible. It may require the less biased aid of psychological testing or of personal analysis by those trained to do so. More often it takes only the honesty to admit where one's strengths do and do not lie, even in one's subject matter where the presumption is that he knows a great deal about all aspects of it.

After the inventory process is completed, the teacher may well decide that he is lacking in certain strengths which would take a long, long time to develop. We suggested earlier in this chapter that no man can fight all the necessary battles of mankind; it is a matter of priorities. In some cases one may have the requisite strengths to lead a fight, in others, the skills to aid or follow, and in still others, one may simply have to admit to oneself that the best he can do at present is just to stay out of the way!

This in no way should be construed to mean that one who *has* grave weaknesses and *recognizes* them to be undesirable in himself and by himself should merely shrug off those which would take a long time to correct. It is simply to state with Franklin that "Art is long and time is short." No man in his lifetime can serve all causes, so he must establish priorities. He must periodically examine himself and ask with the comedian, "Are you contributing to the solution — or are you part of the problem?"

Probably the most appropriate quotation with which to end this book is the following one from William James: "The greatest use of a life is to spend it for something that will outlast it." It is our belief that to recognize the social problems in the relationships between the school and society is half the battle. The other is to know oneself well enough and bravely enough to serve where and when one can to combat the social ills that one sees. This book is addressed to the first half of the battle; how to realize James' advice in one's own life is a part of the lonesome journey of each of us. But it seems worthy of our best efforts.

SUGGESTIONS FOR FURTHER READING

Bakan, David. *The Duality of Human Existence.* Chicago: Rand McNally & Co., 1966.

Beck, Carlton E. *Guidance in a New Era: An Existential View.* Englewood Cliffs, N.J.: Prentice-Hall, 1968 (in press).

Becker, Ernest. *Beyond Alienation.* New York: George Braziller, 1967.

Bugental, J. F. T. *The Search for Authenticity.* New York: Holt, Rinehart & Winston, 1963.

Hamachek, Don E. *The Self in Growth, Teaching, and Learning.* Englewood Cliffs, N.J.: Prentice-Hall, 1965.

Jourard, Sidney M. *Personal Adjustment.* New York: The Macmillan Co., 1958.

Keniston, Kenneth. *The Uncommitted.* New York: Harcourt, Brace & World, 1965.

Wheelis, Allen. *The Quest for Identity.* New York: W. W. Norton & Company, 1958.

Photograph Acknowledgments

Page 100   National Gallery of Art, Washington, D.C., Rosen-
            wald Collection
Page 113   George Eastman House, Photographs by Lewis W.
            Hine
Page 117   *top:* Ken Heyman
            middle: Library of Congress
Page 121   General Dynamics
Page 126   John Moss, Black Star
Page 133   Brown Brothers
Page 134   Israel Information Services
Page 137   *top:* Housing and Home Finance Agency, Office of
            Public Affairs
            bottom: Charles S. Rice
Page 140   Brown Brothers
Page 144   United Press International Photo
Page 154   Photo by Paul Conklin, Peace Corps
Page 163   *top:* National Film Board, photo by C. Wilkinson
            bottom: John C. Goodwin
Page 168   *top:* International Communication Films
            bottom: Photo by Paul Conklin, Peace Corps
Page 169   *top:* Photo by Carl Purcell, Peace Corps
            middle: International Communications Films
            bottom: Goskin Sipahioglu, Black Star
Page 175   Eric L. Brown
Page 176   Museum of Science, Boston
Page 181   Ken Heyman
Page 183   *top:* Photo by James Foote
            bottom: Job Corps
Page 185   Photo by Paul Conklin, Teachers' Corps
Page 193   Stephen Filipowski
Page 206   Elizabeth Wilcox
Page 210   Harvard Graduate School of Education
Page 219   *top:* National Education Association, Carl Purcell
            middle: National Education Association, Carl Purcell
            bottom: Tom Wills
Page 231   National Education Association, Carl Purcell
Page 232   E. I. Du Pont de Nemours & Co., Inc.
Page 235   Photo by Joan Larson, Vista
Page 240   Patricia Hollander
Page 247   Eric L. Brown

Index of Names

251

General Index